Holly Clegg's trim&TERRIFIC™

KITCHEN 101

Enjoy my book
Holly Clegg

Secrets to Cooking Confidence

Library of Congress Control Number: 2012909136
ISBN-13   978-0-9815640-2-9
ISBN-10   0-9815640-2-X

Cover and interior book design by TILT (tiltthis.com)
Edited by Lee Jackson, LDN, RD
Creative consulting by Pamela Clegg Hill
Nutritional Analysis: Tammi Hancock, Hancock Nutrition

Other Books by Holly Clegg:

Holly Clegg's trim&TERRIFIC® Too Hot in the Kitchen
Holly Clegg's trim&TERRIFIC® Gulf Coast Favorites
Holly Clegg trim&TERRIFIC® Freezer Friendly Meals
Holly Clegg trim&TERRIFIC® Diabetic Cooking
Eating Well Through Cancer: Easy Recipes & Recommendations Before & After Treatment

To order books, call **1-800-88HOLLY** or visit **hollyclegg.com** or **thehealthycookingblog.com**

Production and Manufacturing:
Favorite Recipes Press
An imprint of FRP
P.O. Box 305142
Nashville, TN 37230
800-358-0560

On the front cover: Chipotle Chicken Tacos with Avocado Salsa (pg 110)

On the title page: BBQ Shrimp Tacos (pg 118), Meaty Lasagna (pg 158), Chocolate Chip Peanut Butter Oatmeal Cookie (pg 177), Southwestern Cole Slaw (pg 120)

On the back cover: Philly Cheesesteak (pg 25), Caprese Salad (pg 79), Chocolate Peanut Butter Trifle (pg 188-189)

KITCHEN 101

If you're familiar with my trim&TERRIFIC™ cookbook series, you know I strive to include recipes that are delicious, healthy and easy to prepare. Recently, when I was sitting on a plane, the gentleman next to me said, "You should write a book for people at any stage in life ready to begin cooking." I believe I've satisfied that request with the simple, practical and quick recipes found in *KITCHEN 101: Secrets to Cooking Confidence*. Whether you're off to college, your first apartment, getting married, having a family, single or just plain busy, *KITCHEN 101* will help guide you through the kitchen with practical recipes as well as the basic tools and tips you need to cook healthier. My philosophy in this book was to include recipes that are "the easiest of easy" and use the least amount of ingredients to give the recipe the most flavor.

I listened to each and every one of your requests when building the book, including your favorite shortcuts, cooking methods and recipe requests. In the last hour, I added a *Crock Pot Convenience* Chapter, as I've learned slow cooker cooking is a favorite preparation method for many as you can cook without even being home! I also added a *Crock Pot* symbol to help identify crock pot recipes throughout the book. Also, since rotisserie chicken is such a time saver, there is a chapter completely dedicated to using rotisserie chicken called *Rapid Rotisserie Chicken Recipes*. *Start Simple* and *Fix It Fast* are great resources for that last minute meal you desperately need after you've had an overwhelming day. I know many of you like menus as a guide to help put together a well-rounded meal so the *Ready-Made Menus* chapter includes a variety of menus whether you are having a sports get-together or want to impress your guests. *Building on Basics* teaches you

how to prepare and add on to your favorite "fast food pick-ups" (burgers, tacos, pizzas and potatoes). And, no cookbook would be complete without a *Sweet Temptations* chapter which is entirely devoted to satisfying your sweet tooth. Finally, most importantly, *Cooking Basics* is the reference section every cook needs with information from pantry stocking to pan sizes. All of the basics to give you confidence in the kitchen.

Aside from crock pot, vegetarian and freezer-friendly symbols (see list below), I've included a diabetic symbol to indicate *Diabetic Friendly* recipes. My hope is for you to understand a diabetic diet is the healthiest way to eat and doesn't necessarily mean you have to give up your favorites.

 Vegetarian recipes

 Freezer-friendly recipes that you can make ahead

 Crock pot recipes that can be made in a slow cooker

 D Diabetic Friendly recipes that meet the ADA guidelines

Each recipe includes the nutritional analysis and the dietary exchange. The analysis is based on the larger serving.

The nutritional analysis does not include any salt and pepper (since it is listed to taste) or any ingredient with "optional" after it.

*With my mainstream healthier recipes, you can "have your cake and eat it too" as you don't have to change what you eat, just how you prepare it. **KITCHEN 101** accomplishes an overall healthier lifestyle by giving you the recipes, tips and information to cook fabulous, time-efficient meals with everyday ingredients. Hit your kitchen and start cooking!*

KITCHEN 101 is for all those who have stirred my pots through my life!

GROWING UP — **Ruth** and **Jerry**, my parents, my patience (and cooking) comes from my mom and my business drive from my dad, two wonderful role models. When my father was diagnosed with larynx cancer, I wrote my cancer cookbook to help him through a challenging time and ensure that one's love of food isn't hindered by illness, a most fulfilling project. **Mae Mae**, my Baton Rouge mom, she's my food critic, picks up dinner, and my kitchen and life wouldn't be the same without her. **Marcia** and **Selma**, you've always been a food influence in my life for as long as I can remember. **Joyce**, you were my #1 sales agent when I catered and always my official taster.

COLLEGE DORM ROOM COOKING — **Leslie**, **Lila**, **Jolie**, **Sherri** and **Amy** — it all started in Jolie's toaster oven in our dorm. I value your friendships now as much as I did then.

MY LONGTIME NEIGHBORS — **Francine**, a life-long friend, and **Don**, for your fabulous fresh fish. **Gail**, **Lynell** (my groupie), **Clifford's**, **Mockler's**, **Engquist's** and **Sligar's** — sharing fun times, always revolving around food.

WHAT'S FOR DINNER? — The joke in my house is my husband **Mike's** favorite request is, "May I have a simple meal like tuna fish?" Usually, the answer is no that's boring. He's tasted all of my food, stood by my side with encouragement, listened patiently to each and every opportunity, and has been my devoted partner in life. **Todd**, **Sana** and **Lyla** — Todd, my son, I treasure your daily call while walking to Onex and your caring advice outside the kitchen. **Sana**, adoring wife and another daughter to me, knows how to make a small NY kitchen work when she cooks and entertains. Precious **Lyla**, you'll be my kitchen helper soon! **Courtney**, **Chad** and **Baby G** (baby on the way) — Courtney's (my daughter) public relations expertise and Chad's (my Dallas son) unconditional helping hand are invaluable to me professionally and even more as a mother. **Haley**, my baby, cooks as fast and as much as me. I love that she has my passion for food we share together on the phone or in the kitchen. **Dr. Ilene** (sister), we might not share recipes, but that's about all we don't share! Don't ever quit calling with "what to cook" questions as you are my cooking measuring stick.

Dr. Bart, your other expertise keeps me well to cook and you even have kitchen skills. **Pam** (Colorado sis), my foodie traveling companion and cooking counterpart, and I value your willingness to cook and discuss recipes at any time, plus **Jim** gets to enjoy all the recipe testing. **Michael** (my brother), I truly relish our meals and times together, plus you have the best taste in wine. **Jordan**, **Madeline** and **Jacob** — our fun times eating out.

PARTY TIME — **Karen**, I count on you as my partner in eating, drinking, driving Miss Holly, and our life-changing exercise chats. **Louann**, our friendship began over 35 years ago with your Crabmeat au Gratin recipe. **Dr. Ronnie**, you hold the title for the best Blackened Redfish ever. **Terri**, I count on you for good wine and fun times, and of course, food pick-ups. **Gracie**, we share recipes, food trips and our love of food. **Melanie H**, I adore our special lunches and bond.

MY JOB IS COOKING — **Al** and **Nancy**, Diane Allen and the Louisiana Sweet Potato Commission, thanks for years of working together, I love my Louisiana yams! **Mike**, **Avery** and **AJ** at Louisiana Farm Bureau for fun TV tapings. **Melanie**, a friendship that began from diet coke recipes. **Gerald** (and **Melinda**) for being a partner in my most gratifying project and dear friends. **Jill**, for being my first official foodie friend. **Renate** — it began with you at the Cordon Bleu in London.

WRITING COOKBOOKS — **Lee**, my right and left hand, for having an endless job description, and being there to share whatever our latest and greatest opportunity is, and making it better because you are there with me! **Joni**, for witty words and being so dependable. **Karen**, a devoted friend (through sickness and health) and for your creative input at our satellite office (the gym). **Sheila**, at FRP for valued advice plus friendship, food, and fun. **Mike** and **Avery**, for your dependable camera skills and book title input. **Colleen**, always lending a listening ear. **Scott** and **Caroline**, at TILT, for your design skills created an exceptional book, **Tammi**, for years of efficient nutritional information. And finally my **Facebook Fans**, for helping co-create my books, the *Crock Pot* chapter is all because of y'all!

HOW TO SET THE TABLE

1. Dinner plate
2. Napkin
3. Salad fork
4. Fork
5. Knife
6. Teaspoon
7. Soup spoon
8. Salad plate
9. Bread plate
10. Bread knife
11. Dessert spoon
12. Dessert fork
13. Water
14. Wine
15. Cup & Saucer

- *The setting above may show more plates and silverware than you need: just remove the extra pieces.*
- *If you are serving, always serve from the left and remove dishes from the right.*

1

COOKING BASICS

KITCHEN STOCK

COOKING UTENSILS: Heat resistant and nonstick spatulas

KNIVES: Paring knife, serrated knife and 8-10" chef knife

MEASURING CUPS AND SPOONS: Various sizes and glass measuring cups with spout, for liquids

MIXING UTENSILS: Hand held or stand-alone electric mixer and wire whisk

NONSTICK COOKWARE

2, 4, and 8-quart pots with covers

6 or 8' and 12" skillet with cover

Two or three 9" round cake pans

9" square cake pan

13"x9"x2" baking pan

9"x5"x3" loaf pan

Bundt pan

9" pie pan

12 cup muffin pan

Cooling racks

Two baking pans (cookies)

KITCHEN GADGETS

Blender

Can opener

Colander

Corkscrew (definitely)

Food processor

Garlic press

Grater

Kitchen scissors

Meat thermometer

Mixer (stand alone or hand)

Pot holders

Pizza cutter

Toaster oven

Vegetable peeler

PANTRY SHOPPING LIST

REFRIGERATOR STAPLES

Bell peppers (red, yellow, green)

Biscuits, crescent rolls, pizza crust

Butter

Cheese (varieties/reduced-fat)

Cream cheese (reduced-fat)

Eggs

Fruit

Garlic (minced in jar, fresh)

Jalepeños in jar (diced or sliced)

Lemon and lime juice

Milk (skim)

Mixed greens (baby spinach)

Onion (yellow, red, and green)

Sour Cream (fat-free or light)

Vegetables

Yogurt, Greek and plain (nonfat or light)

PANTRY STAPLES

Biscuit baking mix

Bread (whole wheat or white)

Bread crumbs (Italian, plain, panko)

Couscous

Dried cranberries

Evaporated skimmed milk

Oils (canola, olive, sesame)

Pasta: assorted shapes and flavors

Rice (white, brown, wild, Arborio)

BAKING STAPLES

Baking powder

Baking soda

Cake mixes (chocolate, yellow, brownie)

Chocolate chips (dark, and semisweet)

Cocoa

Cornstarch

Extracts (vanilla, almond, butter, and coconut)

Flour (all-purpose, whole wheat)

Instant pudding and pie filling

Nonstick cooking spray

Nuts

Oatmeal (old-fashioned)

Sugar (granulated, brown and confectioners')

Sweetened condensed milk (fat-free)

CONDIMENT STAPLES

Honey

Hot sauce

Ketchup

Marinara sauces (jars)

Mayonnaise (light or low fat)

Mustard (creole, Dijon or yellow)

Salad dressing (fat-free or reduced-fat)

Salsa

Soy sauce (low-sodium)

Vinegar (balsamic, seasoned rice, white, and wine)

Worcestershire sauce

CANNED GOODS

Artichokes

Beans (assorted)

Broth (beef, chicken, vegetable)

Diced tomatoes and green chilies

Enchilada sauce

Green chilies (diced)

Olives (Kalamata sliced)

Tomatoes (diced, paste, sauce)

Water chestnuts (sliced)

SPICE PANTRY STARTER LIST

Basil leaves

Chili powder

Cinnamon (ground)

Cumin (ground)

Dill weed leaves

Garlic powder

Ginger (ground)

Italian blend

Oregano leaves

Paprika

Parsley flakes (dried)

Pepper (black, coarsely ground, red pepper flakes)

Poppy seeds

Salt

Sesame seeds

Thyme leaves

FROZEN PANTRY STAPLES

Chicken breasts

Fish

Frozen veggies (spinach, corn, edamame...)

Meat (flank steak, brisket)

Pork tenderloins

Shrimp

Sirloin (ground, roast)

Yogurt or Ice cream (reduced-fat or fat-free)

CULINARY DICTIONARY

Bake: To cook food, covered or uncovered using an oven. Usually refers to cakes, cookies, desserts and casseroles.

Baste: To moisten foods during cooking with pan drippings or sauce to enhance flavor and prevent drying.

Beat: To make mixture smooth by whipping in mixer or briskly with wire whisk.

Blanch: To plunge food into boiling water for a brief time to preserve color, nutritional value or great for loosening skins of tomatoes or peaches and making crisp tender veggies.

Blend: To combine two or more ingredients until smooth and uniform in texture, flavor and color. Use a mixer or by hand.

Boil: To heat liquid until bubbles form continuously, rise in a steady pattern, and break the surface.

Broil: To cook food a certain distance directly under dry heat. Indoor version of grilling.

Caramelize: To melt sugar slowly over low heat until it becomes a golden brown, caramel-flavored syrup.

Chop: Cut into coarse or fine irregular pieces, using knife or food processor.

Coat: Cover food evenly with crumbs or sauce.

Cream: To beat a mixture consisting usually of butter and sugar to a light fluffy consistency. This process incorporates air into the mixture so baked products have a lighter texture.

Cube: To cut food into uniform pieces, usually 1/2 inch or larger, using knife.

Cut in: To work a solid fat (butter) into dry ingredients usually with pastry blender or two knives in a crisscross motion until coarse crumbs form.

Dash: Less than 1/8 teaspoon of an ingredient.

Dice: Cut food into squares smaller than 1/2 inch, using knife.

Dissolve: To stir a dry ingredient into a liquid ingredient until the dry ingredient disappears.

Drizzle: Gradually pour topping in thin lines in an uneven pattern over food.

Flake: To gently break a food into small pieces using a fork (refers to fish).

Fold: Gently combine a lighter mixture with a heavier mixture by using a circular motion bringing contents of a bowl to top with spatula.

Glaze: A thin glossy coating on a food.

Grate: To rub a hard textured food against the small rough, sharp-edged holes of a grater (cheese).

Grease: To coat surface with a thin layer of fat or oil. Nonstick cooking spray may be used.

Julienne: To cut food into thin match-like sticks about two inches long.

Marinade: A savory liquid in which food is placed in to add flavor and tenderize. Marinate refers to the process.

Mash: To press or beat a food to remove lumps and make a smooth mixture.

Mince: To cut food into very fine pieces, smaller than chopped.

Pare: To cut off skin or outer covering of a fruit or vegetable using a small knife or vegetable peeler.

Partially set: A mixture is chilled to a consistency of unbeaten egg whites. Other ingredients are added at this stage so they will stay evenly distributed and not sink to bottom or float.

Peel: To cut off outer covering or skin of a vegetable or fruit.

Poach: To cook in simmering liquid just below boiling point.

Preheat: To heat an oven to specific temperature before using it.

Puree: To change a solid food into a liquid or heavy paste, usually by using a blender or food processor.

Reconstitute: To bring a concentrate or condensed food to its original strength by adding water.

Reduce: To rapidly boil liquid uncovered so some of the liquid evaporates and intensifies the flavor.

Rind: The skin or outer coating of food (citrus fruits, watermelon, cheese).

Roast: To cook with a dry heat cooking method (no liquid) used for meats, poultry, and vegetables that are cooked, uncovered in an oven.

Roux: A French term that refers to a mixture of flour and a fat (oil) cooked to a golden or rich brown color and used for thickening in sauces, soups, and gumbos.

Sauté: To cook or brown food in small amount of hot fat with frequent tossing or turning motion.

Scald: To heat liquid to just below boiling point. Tiny bubbles will form at edge and thin skin will form on top of milk.

Sear: To brown food quickly on all sides using high heat to seal in juices.

Shred: To cut into long thin pieces using round smooth holes of shredder.

Simmer: To cook a food in liquid on low heat that is kept just below the boiling point. Bubbles will rise slowly and break just below the surface.

Skim: To remove a substance such as fat or foam from the surface of a liquid.

Slice: To cut food into uniform size flat thin pieces.

Soften: To let cold food stand at room temperature before using (butter, cream cheese).

Steam: To cook food by placing on a rack or in steamer basket over small amount of boiling water as vapor given off by boiling water cooks food. Steaming helps retain flavor, shape, color, texture, and nutritional value.

Stew: To cook food in liquid for long time until tender in covered pot.

Stir: To mix ingredients with spoon or utensil to combine to prevent food from sticking during cooking or to cool food after cooking.

Stiff peaks: To beat egg whites until peaks stand up straight when beaters are lifted from bowl, while still moist and glossy.

Stir-Fry: An Oriental method of quickly cooking small pieces of food in hot oil over high heat, stirring constantly.

Strain: To pour mixture or liquid through fine sieve or strainer to remove larger pieces.

Toss: To mix ingredients lightly by lifting and dropping them with two utensils (salad greens).

Whip: To beat food lightly and rapidly using a wire whisk or mixer to incorporate air into mixture and increase its volume.

Zest: The colored outer portion of citrus fruit peel which is used to add flavor in recipes.

"A well stocked pantry is like a permanent shopping list."

ABOUT HERBS

- 1 teaspoon dried herbs = 1 tablespoon fresh herbs

- Dried or ground herbs begin to lose their flavor about six months after being opened. (Mark purchase date on bottom of container).

- Dried herbs can be added early in recipe preparation as they require longer exposure to heat and moisture to release their flavor.

- Crush dried herbs in your hands before adding to a recipe to better release their flavor.

- Add most fresh herbs at end of recipe preparation so heat doesn't destroy fresh flavor and aroma.

- To revitalize fresh herbs, snip off stem ends and place in a glass of water (about one inch) in refrigerator.

HERB DICTIONARY

Basil: Minty, clove-like flavor and key ingredient in Mediterranean and Italian cooking (pesto and tomato sauces), salads, stews, meats and eggs.

Bay leaf: Woodsy herb, native to the Mediterranean and mostly available dried. Bay leaves are used to flavor soups, stews, sauces, vegetables, and meats. Remove before serving.

Chives: Mild onion flavor available fresh year round. Best to add at end of cooking to retain their flavor. Used to flavor appetizers, soups, eggs, and salads.

Cilantro: Also known as fresh coriander or Chinese parsley, cilantro has distinct aromatic flavor used in Asian, Caribbean, and Latin American cooking. Available year round in grocery stores and looks like parsley so check carefully.

Dill weed: Delicate taste with tangy lemony flavor. Use with fish, seafood, salads, egg dishes, breads, sauces, and vegetables. Fresh dill leaves are available in late summer and early fall.

Mint: Peppermint has sharp pungent flavor; spearmint is more delicate. Both have a sweet, refreshing flavor and cool aftertaste. Mint is available year round but more plentiful in the summer months. Mint is used to flavor sauces, vegetables, jelly, fruits, and alcoholic beverages.

Oregano: Belongs to mint family and has robust pungent flavor and aroma. Great with pizza or any Italian dish, soups, and tomato based dishes, sauces, vegetables and chicken.

Parsley: Slightly peppery fresh flavored herb used as garnish and mild flavoring. The two varieties are curly-leaf which is used more in garnishing and flat leaf or Italian is more strongly flavored and used in cooking.

Rosemary: Highly aromatic with bold flavor and hints of both lemon and pine. Delicious sprinkled over any roasted meat, poultry, tomato based dishes, seafoods, stuffings and soups.

Tarragon: Has spicy, sharp flavor with licorice overtones and is essential to classic French cooking. Use sparingly as can have a dominant flavor.

Thyme: Minty, yet lemony aroma. Thyme is used to season poultry, meat, vegetables, fish dishes and soups. Available dried either ground or in leaves.

About salad greens:
1 pound salad greens = 6 cups torn

Chicken Fajita Pizza (pg 102)

Easy Cinnamon Rolls (pg 17)

2

START SIMPLE

BEST BANANA BREAD

Biscuit baking mix keeps the recipe simple, cream cheese gives it a rich flavor and ripe bananas make it moist; an exceptional quick bread. Of course, I always include nuts!

Makes 16 slices

4 ounces reduced-fat cream cheese

3/4 cup light brown sugar

2 eggs

1 1/2 cups mashed bananas

1 3/4 cups biscuit baking mix

1 teaspoon ground cinnamon

1 cup chopped pecans or walnuts, optional

1 Preheat oven 350°F. Coat 9 x 5 x 3-inch loaf pan with nonstick cooking spray.

2 In large mixing bowl, mix together cream cheese and brown sugar until light and fluffy. Beat in eggs and bananas. Stir in biscuit mix, cinnamon and nuts, if using until just blended. Transfer to prepared pan.

3 Bake 40-45 minutes or until toothpick inserted in center comes out clean.

NUTRITIONAL INFO:

Calories 138

Calories from Fat 25%

Fat 4g

Saturated Fat 2g

Cholesterol 28mg

Sodium 205mg

Carbohydrates 24g

Dietary Fiber 1g

Total Sugars 13g

Protein 3g

Dietary Exchanges:
1 starch, 1/2 fruit, 1/2 fat

TERRIFIC TIP

Have over-ripe bananas? Freeze to pull out and make banana bread at any time. Freeze with or without peeling in plastic freezer zip-top bags.

EASY CINNAMON ROLLS

Keep canned biscuits handy to make this fast and fabulous treat.

  D

Makes 10 rolls

1 (10-biscuit) can refrigerated biscuits or whole wheat biscuits

2 tablespoons butter

1 tablespoon sugar

1 teaspoon ground cinnamon

1/4 cup chopped pecans, optional

1 Preheat oven 425°F. Coat 15x10x1-inch baking sheet with nonstick cooking spray.

2 Flatten each biscuit with your hand or rolling pin. Spread each biscuit with butter.

3 In small bowl, combine sugar and cinnamon together. Sprinkle cinnamon mixture on top of butter; sprinkle with pecans, if desired.

4 Roll up each biscuit like a cigar and form a circle by putting the ends together. Bake 8-10 minutes or until golden brown.

NUTRITIONAL INFO:

Calories 76

Calories from Fat 35%

Fat 3g

Saturated Fat 1g

Cholesterol 6mg

Sodium 210mg

Carbohydrates 11g

Dietary Fiber 0g

Total Sugars 3g

Protein 1g

Dietary Exchanges:
1 starch, 1/2 fat

PULL APART ITALIAN BREAD

Simple and most amazing buttery tasting bread. Can omit Italian seasoning if desired.

Makes 12-16 servings

3 tablespoons butter, melted

3 (8-ounce) cans reduced-fat crescent rolls

2 teaspoons Italian blend seasoning

1 Preheat oven 375°F.

2 Pour butter into bottom of nonstick Bundt pan. Unroll crescent rolls into four rectangles (two triangular shapes) and roll up (like cigar). Layer on top the butter, sprinkle seasoning between layers. Layers will overlap and don't have to be exact.

3 Bake 19-23 minutes or until top is golden brown. Immediately invert onto serving plate.

NUTRITIONAL INFO:
Calories 156
Calories from Fat 49%
Fat 9g
Saturated Fat 4g
Cholesterol 6mg
Sodium 353mg
Carbohydrates 18g
Dietary Fiber 0g
Total Sugars 3g
Protein 3g
Dietary Exchanges:
1 starch, 2 fat

ARTICHOKE HUMMUS

 D

Liven up hummus with this simple addition of artichokes.

Makes 8 (1/4-cup) servings

1 (14-ounce) can artichoke hearts, drained

1 (15-ounce) can Great Northern beans, rinsed and drained

2 tablespoons lemon juice

1 1/2 teaspoons minced garlic

1 teaspoon sesame oil

1 In food processor or blender, mix all ingredients.

NUTRITIONAL INFO:
Calories 54
Calories from Fat 10%
Fat 1g
Saturated Fat 0g
Cholesterol 0mg
Sodium 141mg
Carbohydrates 9g
Dietary Fiber 2g
Total Sugars 2g
Protein 3g
Dietary Exchanges:
1/2 starch

Pull Apart Italian Bread

Artichoke Hummus

TACO DIP

This popular taco-style dip makes a fast group favorite. Sprinkle with cheese and black olives, if desired. Serve with chips.

Makes 16 (1/4-cup) servings

1 pound ground sirloin

4 ounces reduced-fat cream cheese

1 cup nonfat sour cream

1/2 cup chopped green onions

1 (1.25-ounce) packet taco seasoning

1 1/2 cups salsa

1 cup chopped tomato

1/2 cup chopped avocado

1 In large nonstick skillet, cook meat until done; drain excess grease. Add remaining ingredients except tomato and avocado, cooking until mixture is creamy and cheese is melted

2 Transfer mixture to serving dish. Top with chopped tomato and avocado. Serve warm.

NUTRITIONAL INFO:

Calories 95

Calories from Fat 36%

Fat 4g

Saturated Fat 2g

Cholesterol 23mg

Sodium 286mg

Carbohydrates 7g

Dietary Fiber 1g

Total Sugars 2g

Protein 8g

Dietary Exchanges:
1/2 other carbohydrate,
1 lean meat

TERRIFIC TIP

In crock pot, add cooked meat and remaining ingredients except tomato and avocado; add just before serving.

OLIVE PARMESAN CHEESE BITES

 D

NUTRITIONAL INFO:

Calories 56

Calories from Fat 34%

Fat 2g

Saturated Fat 0g

Cholesterol 2mg

Sodium 189mg

Carbohydrates 7g

Dietary Fiber 0g

Total Sugars 1g

Protein 2g

Dietary Exchanges:
1/2 starch, 1/2 fat

TERRIFIC TIP

Olive tapenade can be found in the pickle/olive aisle of the grocery store, as it is simply a blend of several types of olives and spices in a spreading consistency.

In a pinch raid the olive bar and chop olives in food processor.

Grab a can of pizza dough, spread with pre-made olive mixture and Parmesan cheese for an instant incredible pick-up. Refrigerate leftovers and reheat in oven.

Makes 28 bites

1 (10-13.8-ounce) can refrigerated pizza crust dough

1/2 cup olive tapenade

2/3 cup grated Parmesan cheese

1 Preheat oven 450°F. Coat baking pan with nonstick cooking spray.

2 Unroll pizza crust dough and spread olive tapenade over dough, leaving 1/4-inch border. Sprinkle with cheese. Cut dough across in middle to make two rectangles.

3 Carefully roll up each rectangular piece of dough, starting at long side. Cut into 1-inch slices. Place slices in prepared pan. Coat top with nonstick cooking spray. Bake 10-12 minutes or until golden. Remove from pan and serve immediately.

QUICK CHILI

I needed a last minute dinner so I took ground beef from the freezer and raided my pantry to make this fantastic quick full-flavored chili. Serve with chopped red onions, avocado and shredded reduced-fat cheese.

Makes 4 heaping (1-cup) servings

1 pound ground sirloin

1 onion, chopped

1 (15-ounce) can fat-free chicken broth

1 (10 1/2-ounce) can diced tomatoes and green chilies

1 (6-ounce) can tomato paste

1 tablespoon chili powder

1/4 teaspoon ground cumin

Dash ground cinnamon

Salt and pepper to taste

1 (15-ounce) can black beans, drained and rinsed

1 In large nonstick pot, cook meat and onion until done; drain off any excess fat.

2 Add remaining ingredients and bring to a boil. Reduce heat, and cook over low heat about 10 minutes.

NUTRITIONAL INFO:

Calories 318

Calories from Fat 20%

Fat 7g

Saturated Fat 2g

Cholesterol 62mg

Sodium 759mg

Carbohydrates 31g

Dietary Fiber 11g

Total Sugars 9g

Protein 34g

Dietary Exchanges:
1 starch, 3 vegetable, 4 lean meat

TERRIFIC TIP

To cook in slow cooker, first cook meat and onion in skillet until done.

SPICY GLAZED CHICKEN

 D

In the oven or on the grill, this spicy rub with a honey glaze turns chicken into a quick amazing meal.

Makes 4 (4-ounce) servings

1 teaspoon chili powder

2 teaspoons paprika

2 teaspoons garlic powder

1/2 teaspoon red pepper flakes

Salt and pepper to taste

1 pound boneless skinless chicken breasts

1/3 cup honey

1 tablespoon apple cider vinegar

1 Preheat broiler. Cover baking sheet with foil.

2 In small bowl, mix together chili powder, paprika, garlic powder, red pepper flakes and season to taste. Coat chicken with rub mixture and transfer to prepared pan. Broil 5 minutes on each side (can grill) or until chicken is done.

3 In small bowl, mix honey and vinegar. Turn chicken again and baste or coat with honey mixture, cooking a few minutes or until honey starts to thicken and forms a glaze (may smoke a little).

NUTRITIONAL INFO:

Calories 228

Calories from Fat 13%

Fat 3g

Saturated Fat 1g

Cholesterol 73mg

Sodium 146mg

Carbohydrates 26g

Dietary Fiber 1g

Total Sugars 24g

Protein 25g

Dietary Exchanges:
1 1/2 other carbohydrate, 3 lean meat

TERRIFIC TIP

Don't buy extra vinegar, whatever you have will work.

SMOTHERED CHICKEN

Effortless flavorsome chicken in a rich brown gravy served over rice is the ultimate comfort food. When done, leave on simmer until ready to serve, you can't overcook — just gets more tender.

Makes 6 servings

1 onion, chopped

1 teaspoon minced garlic

1/2 cup water

2 pounds boneless skinless chicken breasts

1/4 cup all-purpose flour dissolved in 1/2 cup water

1 cup fat-free chicken broth

1 bunch green onions, chopped

2 tablespoons chopped parsley

Salt and pepper to taste

1 In large nonstick skillet coated with nonstick cooking spray, sauté onion and garlic until tender and browned, 5–7 minutes. Add 1/2 cup water and continue cooking 5 minutes.

2 Add chicken. Bring to boil, reduce heat, cover and cook 20-30 minutes until chicken is tender.

3 In small cup mix together flour and water and add to skillet, stirring until smooth and thickens. Gradually add broth, cooking until chicken is done and gravy is bubbling, another 15-20 minutes.

4 Stir in green onions, parsley, and season to taste.

  D

NUTRITIONAL INFO:

Calories 216

Calories from Fat 18%

Fat 4g

Saturated Fat 1g

Cholesterol 97mg

Sodium 249mg

Carbohydrates 9g

Dietary Fiber 2g

Total Sugars 3g

Protein 33g

Dietary Exchanges:
1/2 starch, 1 vegetable, 4 lean meat

TERRIFIC TIP

If you're only using a small amount of parsley, dried parsley is fine.

FANTASTIC FLANK STEAK

Marinade is the key to adding flavor to flank steak. For a terrific quick meal this is a go-to marinade. Flat iron steak may also be used.

Makes 6 (4-ounce) servings

3 tablespoons low-sodium soy sauce

3 tablespoons honey

1 1/2 teaspoons garlic powder

1/2 teaspoon ground ginger or 1 1/2 teaspoons chopped fresh ginger

1 green onion, chopped

2 tablespoons sherry, optional

2 pounds flank steak, trimmed of excess fat

1 In large plastic bag or glass dish, mix together all ingredients except flank steak. Add flank steak, refrigerate, and marinate 2 hours or time permitted, turning occasionally.

2 Discard marinade. Grill flank steak over hot fire until cooked rare to medium rare, 4-7 minutes on each side. May be broiled in oven. Serve rare, let sit 5 minutes before slicing. Cut diagonally across grain into thin slices.

NUTRITIONAL INFO:

Calories 219

Calories from Fat 37%

Fat 9g

Saturated Fat 4g

Cholesterol 64mg

Sodium 250mg

Carbohydrates 1g

Dietary Fiber 0g

Total Sugars 1g

Protein 32g

Dietary Exchanges:
4 lean meat

TERRIFIC TIP

I keep a bottle of pantry-friendly cooking sherry at all times for easy flavor.

PHILLY CHEESESTEAK

One of those outrageously delicious and easy sandwiches that just uses gravy mix and deli meat.

Makes 4 (about 1/3-cup meat) cheesesteaks

1 (1-ounce) packet brown gravy mix

1/2 pound shaved deli roast beef

1 small onion, thinly sliced

Half green pepper, seeded and thinly sliced

3 slices provolone or Swiss cheese, shredded or thinly sliced

4 buns or rolls

1 In nonstick small pot, prepare gravy mix according to directions. When gravy thickens, add roast beef.

2 Meanwhile, in medium nonstick skillet coated with nonstick cooking spray, sauté onion and green pepper until tender, about 5-7 minutes.

3 Split open rolls and place cheese on one side; toast until cheese is melted. After toasted, place about heaping 1/3 cup meat mixture onto bottom of roll. Top with sliced green pepper and onion and replace other half of roll.

NUTRITIONAL INFO:

Calories 286

Calories from Fat 30%

Fat 10g

Saturated Fat 4g

Cholesterol 42mg

Sodium 1011mg

Carbohydrates 30g

Dietary Fiber 2g

Total Sugars 5g

Protein 21g

Dietary Exchanges:
2 starch, 2 lean meat, 1/2 fat

TERRIFIC TIP

Can be served in crock pot to keep warm.

GLAZED PORK TENDERLOIN

 D

NUTRITIONAL INFO:

Calories 241

Calories from Fat 27%

Fat 7g

Saturated Fat 2g

Cholesterol 100mg

Sodium 143mg

Carbohydrates 10g

Dietary Fiber 1g

Total Sugars 7g

Protein 33g

Dietary Exchanges:
1/2 other carbohydrate,
4 lean meat

I promise it's worth buying fig preserves as you'll repeat this recipe often. The combination of sweet figs, fiery chili powder, soy sauce and tart vinegar makes an intoxicating marinade. Cook in the oven or grill — either way this is a hit.

Makes 6 (4-ounce) servings

1/3 cup fig preserves

1 tablespoon chili powder

1 teaspoon minced garlic

2 tablespoons seasoned rice vinegar

1 tablespoon low-sodium soy sauce

2 (1-pound) pork tenderloins, trimmed

Salt and pepper to taste

1 In plastic resealable bag, combine fig preserves, chili powder, garlic, vinegar, and soy sauce. Season tenderloins to taste and place in bag. Refrigerate one hour or longer, time permitted.

2 Preheat oven 350°F. Place tenderloin on baking sheet covered with foil. Cover tenderloins with some of the marinade, toss out remaining marinade.

3 Cook tenderloins, basting after 20 minutes with marinade in pan and continue cooking another 20 minutes or until thickest part of tenderloin registers 160°F.

GLAZED SALMON

If you've never had salmon, here's' my #1 easy and favorite recipe; rumor is this is the best salmon ever! The glaze on the crispy, crusted salmon takes only minutes to prepare — and to disappear from the plate.

Makes 4 servings

1/4 cup honey

2 tablespoons low-sodium soy sauce

2 tablespoons lime juice

1 tablespoon Dijon mustard

4 (6-ounce) salmon fillets

1 In small bowl, whisk together honey, soy sauce, lime juice, and mustard. Marinate salmon in sauce in refrigerator several hours, or time permitted (Do not discard marinade).

2 In nonstick skillet coated with nonstick cooking spray, cook salmon on each side, 3-5 minutes, until golden brown, crispy, and just cooked through. Transfer salmon to platter.

3 Add remaining honey glaze to skillet, and simmer, stirring, until mixture comes to boil. Return salmon to pan, heat thoroughly, and serve immediately.

D

NUTRITIONAL INFO:

Calories 297

Calories from Fat 24%

Fat 8g

Saturated Fat 1g

Cholesterol 80mg

Sodium 403mg

Carbohydrates 20g

Dietary Fiber 0g

Total Sugars 19g

Protein 36g

Dietary Exchanges:
1 1/2 other carbohydrate, 5 lean meat

TERRIFIC TIP

Whenever I need to marinate anything, I always use a plastic bag for easy cleanup.

STUFFED ARTICHOKE CASSEROLE

No fuss with stuffing this artichoke! Mix all the ingredients in one skillet, close your eyes and you will think you are eating a stuffed artichoke. Outstanding and so simple!

Makes 4 (1-cup) servings

1 tablespoon olive oil

1 large onion, chopped

1 teaspoon minced garlic

2 1/2 cups seasoned stuffing mix

1 teaspoon dried oregano leaves

1 teaspoon dried basil leaves

1 cup fat-free chicken broth

1 (14-ounce) can artichoke hearts, drained and coarsely chopped

1/4-1/3 cup grated Parmesan cheese

1 In large nonstick skillet, heat oil and sauté onion and garlic until tender. Add stuffing, oregano and basil, mixing until combined. Add chicken broth and artichokes, carefully mixing.

2 Add cheese stirring until heated and well mixed.

NUTRITIONAL INFO:

Calories 216
Calories from Fat 39%
Fat 10g
Saturated Fat 3g
Cholesterol 6mg
Sodium 759mg
Carbohydrates 26g
Dietary Fiber 3g
Total Sugars 5g
Protein 7g
Dietary Exchanges:
1 starch, 2 vegetable, 2 fat

TERRIFIC TIP

Prepare ahead of time and transfer to baking dish. Heat in 350°F. oven 20 minutes or until heated.

For vegetarian version, substitute vegetable broth.

EASY EGGPLANT PARMESAN

Don't be intimidated by this classic Italian dish —
as this version is super easy and super delicious!

Makes 6 servings

2 medium eggplants, peeled and cut in 1/2-inch
   slices (about 1 1/2 pounds)

2 onions, thinly sliced into rings

1 (26-ounce) jar marinara sauce

1 teaspoon dried oregano leaves

1 teaspoon dried basil leaves

1 1/2 cups shredded part-skim mozzarella cheese

1 Preheat oven 350°F. Coat oblong 2-quart baking dish with
   nonstick cooking spray.

2 Arrange eggplant slices along bottom of dish. Top with onions.

3 In large bowl, mix marinara sauce, oregano and basil.
   Spread evenly over onion slices.

4 Bake 40-45 minutes or until eggplant is tender. Sprinkle
   with mozzarella cheese and return to oven 10 minutes
   more or until cheese is melted.

NUTRITIONAL INFO:

Calories 221

Calories from Fat 37%

Fat 9g

Saturated Fat 4g

Cholesterol 15mg

Sodium 634mg

Carbohydrates 26g

Dietary Fiber 7g

Total Sugars 14g

Protein 10g

Dietary Exchanges:
1 starch, 2 vegetable,
1 lean meat, 1 fat

TERRIFIC TIP

*Use different
flavored marinara
sauces.*

OVEN BAKED RISOTTO

No time consuming stirring to whip up this risotto recipe. Aborio rice is the type of rice used to make risotto.

Makes 5 (1-cup) entrees or 10 (1/2-cup) side servings

2 tablespoons butter, melted

2 1/2 cups fat-free chicken broth

1 cup Arborio rice

1 cup chopped onion

Salt and pepper to taste

1 Preheat oven 400 F°

2 In 13x9x2-inch baking dish, mix together butter, broth, Arborio rice, onion and season to taste.

3 Bake, covered, 35 minutes. Remove from oven and fluff rice with fork.

NUTRITIONAL INFO:

Calories 186

Calories from Fat 24%

Fat 5g

Saturated Fat 3g

Cholesterol 12mg

Sodium 506mg

Carbohydrates 32g

Dietary Fiber 1g

Total Sugars 2g

Protein 3g

Dietary Exchanges:
2 starch, 1/2 fat

D

NUTRITIONAL INFO:
As side: 10 (1/2-cup) servings

Calories 93

Calories from Fat 24%

Fat 2g

Saturated Fat 1g

Cholesterol 6mg

Sodium 253mg

Carbohydrates 16g

Dietary Fiber 1g

Total Sugars 1g

Protein 2g

Dietary Exchanges:
1 starch

TERRIFIC TIP

For a delicious option, after risotto is cooked add fresh mozzarella, tomatoes, fresh basil and even chicken.

CORN PUDDING

A quick and tasty comforting combination that will add to any meal.

Makes 8 servings

2 tablespoons canola oil

1 egg

1/2 cup skim milk

1/2 cup chopped onions

1/2 cup chopped green onions

1 1/2 cups frozen corn, thawed

1 (15-ounce) can cream-style corn

1 (8 1/2-ounce) box corn muffin mix

1 Preheat oven 350°F. Coat 9x9x2-inch baking dish with nonstick cooking spray.

2 In large bowl, mix together oil, egg, and milk until blended. Stir in remaining ingredients.

3 Transfer to prepared pan. Bake 45-55 minutes or until mixture is set and golden brown on top.

NUTRITIONAL INFO:

Calories 233

Calories from Fat 26%

Fat 7g

Saturated Fat 1g

Cholesterol 24mg

Sodium 446mg

Carbohydrates 40g

Dietary Fiber 3g

Total Sugars 10g

Protein 5g

Dietary Exchanges:
2 1/2 starch, 1 fat

TERRIFIC TIP

You can use canned corn instead of frozen if you like, but I prefer keeping frozen on hand for its taste and consistency.

BUTTER PECAN ROASTED SWEET POTATOES

Easier than a sweet potato casserole but with the same sweet flavors — candied yams at their finest with a surprise of cayenne to add just a slight kick!

Makes 8 (1/2-cup) servings

6 cups peeled Louisiana yam (sweet potato) cubes (about 1/2-inch)

2 tablespoons butter, cut into small pieces

2 tablespoons light brown sugar

1/4 cup chopped pecans

1/8 teaspoon cayenne pepper

1 Preheat oven 400°F. Line baking sheet with foil.

2 Spread cubed sweet potatoes evenly on pan. Bake 30-35 minutes, turning potatoes after 20 minutes.

3 Remove from oven and sprinkle with butter, brown sugar, pecans and cayenne pepper. Return to oven and continue baking 10-15 minutes or until sugar is caramelized.

NUTRITIONAL INFO:

Calories 148

Calories from Fat ?%

Fat 5g

Saturated Fat 2g

Cholesterol 8mg

Sodium 81mg

Carbohydrates 24g

Dietary Fiber 3g

Total Sugars 8g

Protein 2g

Dietary Exchanges:
1 1/2 starch, 1/2 fat

PEANUT BUTTER COOKIES

Yes, these simple ingredients create a dynamite peanut butter cookie. Sometimes I add chocolate chips too!

  D

Makes 30 cookies

1 cup crunchy peanut butter

1/2 cup light brown sugar

1 egg

1/2 teaspoon baking soda

1/4 cup chopped peanuts

1 Preheat oven 350°F. Coat baking sheet with nonstick cooking spray.

2 In large bowl, combine peanut butter, brown sugar, egg, and baking soda until well combined. Stir in peanuts.

3 Place dough by teaspoonfuls on nonstick baking sheet and press down with a fork to form ridges. Bake 12–14 minutes or until lightly browned.

NUTRITIONAL INFO:

Calories 73

Calories from Fat 57%

Fat 5g

Saturated Fat 1g

Cholesterol 6mg

Sodium 59mg

Carbohydrates 6g

Dietary Fiber 1g

Total Sugars 4g

Protein 3g

Dietary Exchanges:
1/2 other carbohydrate, 1 fat

TERRIFIC TIP

Use a lightly floured fork to keep fork from sticking to the cookie batter when you make ridges in the cookies.

Slice & Bake Chocolate Chip Cookies (pg 49)

Chicken Schwarma (pg 76)

Cucumber, Mint, & Feta (pg 63)

Creamy Mac & Cheese (pg 48)

Caprese Salad (pg 79)

3

READY-MADE MENUS

Date Night (pg 36)
Special Salad
Cheesy Sauce with Vegetables
Artichoke Couscous
Chicken Marsala
Beer Bread
Almost Better Than Sex Cake

Cook To Impress (pg 41)
Chicken Scallopini
Roasted Broccoli
Pecan Rice
Stuffed Mozzarella French Bread
Bananas Foster Pudding Pie

Comfort Food (pg 46)
Easy Roast
Smothered Chicken
Green Bean Casserole
Creamy Mac & Cheese
Best Biscuits
Slice & Bake Chocolate
Chip Cookies

Sports Spread (pg 50)
Spinach Dip, Assorted Veggies
Cheesy Burger Dip
or Taco Dip
Parmesan Pita Pick-Ups
All American Potato Skins
Ham & Cheese Sliders or Beef Sliders
Ooey Gooey Squares

Fancy Food (pg 55)
Seared Tuna with Avocado
Salsa on Rice Crackers
Marinated Shrimp & Artichokes
Candied Pecan Brie
Crabmeat Brie Dip
Mini Heavenly Cheesecake Bites
with Caramel Topping
Italian Layered Spread

Summer Sensations (pg 61)
Shrimp Salad with
Asian Vinaigrette
Cucumber, Mint & Feta
Strawberry Cheesecake Parfait

Best Basic Barbecue (pg 64)
Cool Coleslaw
Sweet Potato Cornbread
Brisket with Mango
Barbecue Sauce
Baked Beans
S'Mores Cookies

Meatless Monday (pg 68)
Corn Dip
Black Bean Soup
Roasted Tomato & Brie Pasta
Artichoke Bread
No Bake German Chocolate Mounds

Mediterranean Menu (pg 73)
Artichoke Hummus
Chopped Greek Salad
Pork Pitas or
Chicken Schwarma

Italian Feast (pg 77)
Calzones
Caprese Salad
Chicken Parmesan Casserole
Chocolate Italian Cream Cake

Southwestern Soirée (pg 80)
Chile Con Queso
Southwestern Slaw
Easy Beef Enchiladas

Chinese Take Out (pg 83)
Tossed Asian Salad with
Wasabi Vinaigrette
Beef & Broccoli Stir-Fry
Stir-Fry Rice

Louisiana Lagniappe (pg 87)
Yummy Yam Quick Bread
Butter Pecan Roasted
Sweet Potatoes
Crabmeat Brie Dip
Red Beans & Rice
Crab Cakes
Cream Cheese Bread Pudding

Holiday Heros (pg 92)
Cranberry Avocado
Mixed Green Salad
Cranberry Nut Oatmeal Bread
Sweet Potato Casserole
with Praline Topping
Spinach & Artichoke Casserole
Red Velvet Cheesecake
Blonde Brownies

DATE NIGHT

Special Salad (pg 37)

Cheesy Sauce with Vegetables (pg 37)

Artichoke Couscous (pg 38)

Beer Bread (pg 38)

Chicken Marsala (pg 39)

Almost Better Than Sex Cake (pg 40)

Cheesy Sauce with Vegetable

Beer Bread

Chicken Marsala

Almost Better Than Sex Cake

Special Salad

Artichoke Couscous

SPECIAL SALAD

Makes 4 side servings (using about 1/4-1/3-cup vinaigrette)

1 (.6-ounce) package Zesty Italian dressing

1/4 cup vinegar

1/4 cup canola oil

1/4 cup water

1 (9-ounce) package romaine/leafy lettuce (about 6 cups)

1/4 cup grated Parmesan cheese

2 tablespoons sesame seeds, toasted

1 To make vinaigrette, whisk together package Zesty Italian dressing, vinegar, oil and water; set aside.

2 In large bowl, combine lettuce, Parmesan cheese and sesame seeds. Add vinaigrette (about 1/4-1/3 cup, tossing to coat reserving remainder in refrigerator).

NUTRITIONAL INFO:
Calories 114
Calories from Fat 75%
Fat 10g
Saturated Fat 2g
Cholesterol 4mg
Sodium 368mg
Carbohydrates 4g
Dietary Fiber 2g
Total Sugars 2g
Protein 4g
Dietary Exchanges:
2 fat

TERRIFIC TIP *You will have extra vinaigrette for another time. Great salad to build on by adding avocado, tomato or whatever else you want.*

CHEESY SAUCE *with* VEGETABLES

Jazz up your favorite veggie (broccoli, cauliflower, asparagus) with this cheesy sauce.

Makes 5 (1/4-cup) servings

1 tablespoon olive oil

2 tablespoons all-purpose flour

1 cup skim milk

1/2 teaspoon Dijon mustard

1/4 teaspoon garlic powder

1 cup shredded reduced-fat sharp Cheddar cheese

1 In nonstick pot, heat oil and add flour, whisk together until smooth, about 1 minute.

2 Gradually whisk in milk, mustard, and garlic powder into flour mixture. Bring to boil, reduce heat, and cook 3 minutes, stirring until mixture thickens.

3 Add cheese, stirring until melted. Serve with cooked veggie.

NUTRITIONAL INFO:
Calories 109
Calories from Fat 50%
Fat 6g
Saturated Fat 3g
Cholesterol 13mg
Sodium 167mg
Carbohydrates 6g
Dietary Fiber 0g
Total Sugars 2g
Protein 8g
Dietary Exchanges:
1/2 starch, 1 lean meat, 1/2 fat

ARTICHOKE COUSCOUS

 D

Makes 8 (3/4-cup) servings

1 1/2 cups fat-free vegetable or beef broth or water

1/2 teaspoon olive oil

1 1/2 cups couscous

1 onion, chopped

1 teaspoon minced garlic

1 (14-ounce) can artichoke heart quarters, drained

3 tablespoons chopped parsley

3 tablespoons grated Parmesan cheese

NUTRITIONAL INFO:
Calories 153
Calories from Fat 7%
Fat 1g
Saturated Fat 0g
Cholesterol 2mg
Sodium 288mg
Carbohydrates 29g
Dietary Fiber 2g
Total Sugars 2g
Protein 6g
Dietary Exchanges:
1 1/2 starch,
1 vegetable

1 In nonstick pot, bring broth and oil to boil. Add couscous, stir, remove from heat and cover 7 minutes. Fluff with fork and transfer to bowl.

2 In small nonstick skillet coated with nonstick cooking spray, sauté onion and garlic until tender. Add to cooked couscous and stir in artichoke hearts, parsley and cheese, tossing well. Serve warm or room temperature.

BEER BREAD

   D

Makes 12 servings

3 cups all-purpose flour

1 tablespoon baking powder

2 tablespoons sugar

1/2 teaspoon salt

1 (12-ounce) can light beer

2 tablespoons honey

2 tablespoons butter, melted

NUTRITIONAL INFO:
Calories 159
Calories from Fat 13%
Fat 2g
Saturated Fat 1g
Cholesterol 5mg
Sodium 215mg
Carbohydrates 29g
Dietary Fiber 1g
Total Sugars 5g
Protein 3g
Dietary Exchanges:
2 starch

1 Preheat oven 350°F. Coat 9x5x3-inch loaf pan with nonstick cooking spray.

2 In medium bowl, combine flour, baking powder, sugar and salt.

3 Stir in beer and honey (microwave honey 5-10 seconds) into dry ingredients until just mixed. Transfer batter to prepared pan.

4 Bake 50 minutes, or until top is golden brown. Remove from oven and pour melted butter over the top.

CHICKEN MARSALA

Fool-proof, fancy and fantastic. Sure to impress your guests with this quick-cooking recipe.

 D

Makes 4 servings

1 1/2 pounds boneless, skinless chicken breasts or thin cutlets

Salt and pepper to taste

1/3 cup all-purpose flour

3 tablespoons olive oil

1/2 pound sliced mushrooms

1/2 cup Marsala wine

2/3 cup fat-free chicken broth

1/4 cup white wine or sherry

Chopped parsley or chopped green onions

1. Season chicken to taste. Place flour on plate and coat chicken in flour.

2. In large nonstick skillet, heat oil and cook chicken over medium heat until golden brown, 3-4 minutes on each side (may have to do in batches). Remove chicken to plate.

3. To same pan, add mushrooms, Marsala wine, broth and white wine to pan, scraping bits from bottom of pan. Bring to boil, reduce heat, and simmer over low heat 5 minutes, stirring occasionally.

4. Return chicken to pan. Cook another 10-15 minutes or until chicken is done. Sprinkle with parsley or green onions.

NUTRITIONAL INFO:

Calories 376

Calories from Fat 36%

Fat 15g

Saturated Fat 2g

Cholesterol 109mg

Sodium 358mg

Carbohydrates 13g

Dietary Fiber 1g

Total Sugars 3g

Protein 39g

Dietary Exchanges:
1 starch, 5 lean meat

In this recipe, Marsala is a key ingredient, but any time wine is called for in a recipe, chicken broth or any other liquid used in the recipe may be substituted.

For thin chicken breasts: Place plastic wrap over chicken and pound flat using a meat tenderizer/mallet until about a quarter inch thick. You can also buy thin chicken breasts at the grocery.

ALMOST BETTER THAN SEX CAKE

TERRIFIC TIP

Grate chocolate in the food processor — break the chocolate into small chunks and chop with the metal blade using on/off pulses.

When a recipe calls for almond extract be sure to use pure almond extract and not imitation — it really makes a difference!

There is an original "Better Than Sex" cake so this is almost — as it's my trim & terrific version — this easy all-time favorite is made with a cake mix, German chocolate, chocolate chips and an almond glaze.

Makes 16-20 servings

1 (18.25-ounce) box yellow cake mix

2/3 cup plus 1-2 tablespoons skim milk

1/4 cup canola oil

2 eggs

2 egg whites

1 cup nonfat plain yogurt

1 (4-serving) box instant vanilla pudding and pie filling

1 (4-ounce) bar German chocolate, grated

1/3 cup semisweet chocolate chips

1/2 cup chopped pecans

1 cup confectioners' sugar

2 teaspoons almond extract

1. Preheat oven 350°F. Coat 10-inch Bundt pan with nonstick cooking spray.

2. In large mixing bowl, combine cake mix, 2/3 cup milk, oil, eggs, egg whites, yogurt, and vanilla pudding. Beat slightly, only until mixture is combined. Stir in grated chocolate, chocolate chips, and pecans.

3. Pour batter into prepared pan. Bake 40-45 minutes, or until an inserted toothpick comes out clean. Do not overbake. Cool 10 minutes, and invert onto a serving plate.

4. In small bowl, mix together confectioners' sugar, almond extract, and remaining 1-2 tablespoons milk, mixing until well combined. Drizzle over warm cake.

COOK TO IMPRESS

Chicken Scallopini

Pecan Rice

Roasted Broccoli

Bananas Foster Pudding Pie

Stuffed Mozzarella French Bread

CHICKEN SCALLOPINI

Quick and impressive entree.
See page 139

ROASTED BROCCOLI

D

NUTRITIONAL INFO:

Calories 68

Calories from Fat 0%

Fat 5g

Saturated Fat 1g

Cholesterol 1mg

Sodium 46mg

Carbohydrates 4g

Dietary Fiber 2g

Total Sugars 1g

Protein 2g

Dietary Exchanges:
1 vegetable, 1 fat

TERRIFIC TIP

If using fresh lemons, you have lemon rind and if not, leave it out and grab bottled lemon juice.

Pine nuts or any toasted nut may be used.

Lemon, cheese and olive oil tossed with roasted broccoli turn into a snazzy side. Recipe doubles easily and pairs with just about any entrée.

Makes 6 (2/3-cup) servings

4 cups broccoli florets

2 tablespoons olive oil

Salt and pepper to taste

2 tablespoons grated Parmesan cheese

1 tablespoon lemon juice

1 teaspoon lemon rind, optional

2 teaspoons pine nuts, toasted, optional

1. Preheat oven 425°F. Line baking pan with foil.

2. Toss broccoli with oil and season to taste; arrange in single layer on pan. Roast about 20 minutes or until tender and browned around edges.

3. Remove from oven and toss with cheese, lemon juice, lemon rind and pine nuts, if desired.

PECAN RICE

Serve this amazing rice with any meal!

Makes 4 (1-cup) servings

2 teaspoons olive oil

1/2 cup chopped onion

1/2 teaspoon minced garlic

1 cup rice

2 cups fat-free vegetable or chicken broth

1/3 cup white wine

1/4 cup chopped green onions

1/4 cup coarsely chopped pecans, toasted

1 In medium nonstick pot coated with nonstick cooking spray, heat oil and sauté onion and garlic about 5 minutes. Add rice, broth and wine. Bring to boil, reduce heat, cook 20 minutes or until liquid is absorbed. Stir in green onions and pecans.

NUTRITIONAL INFO:

Calories 248

Calories from Fat 26%

Fat 7g

Saturated Fat 1g

Cholesterol 0mg

Sodium 469mg

Carbohydrates 39g

Dietary Fiber 1g

Total Sugars 2g

Protein 5g

Dietary Exchanges:
2 1/2 starch, 1 fat

STUFFED MOZZARELLA *&* ONION BREAD

A fancy bread without all the fuss.

Makes 16 slices

1 (16-ounce) loaf Italian bread

6 tablespoons butter

1/2 cup finely chopped onion

2 teaspoons Dijon mustard

1 teaspoon poppy seeds

Dash hot pepper sauce

1 cup shredded part-skim mozzarella cheese

1 Preheat oven 350°F. Slice bread into slices diagonally, but not cutting through bottom crust.

2 In microwave-safe dish, microwave butter and onion until butter is melted. Stir in mustard, poppy seeds, and hot sauce.

3 Spoon mixture between slices. Sprinkle cheese between each slice and a little on top. Transfer bread to baking sheet, bake 10-15 minutes, or until cheese is melted.

NUTRITIONAL INFO:

Calories 137

Calories from Fat 43%

Fat 7g

Saturated Fat 4g

Cholesterol 16mg

Sodium 260mg

Carbohydrates 15g

Dietary Fiber 1g

Total Sugars 1g

Protein 4g

Dietary Exchanges:
1 starch, 1 fat

BANANAS FOSTER PUDDING PIE

TERRIFIC TIP

*For a step saver:
Use prepared
cookie pie crust.*

*For an amazing
banana ice
cream pie,
my sister
substituted non-
fat frozen vanilla
ice cream for
pudding.*

Looking for a "wow factor" dessert? Simple ingredients, chocolate cookies, bananas, pudding and whipped topping turn into the best banana pie ever!

Makes 8-10 servings

2 cups chocolate cookie crumbs

3 tablespoons melted butter plus 2 tablespoons butter

2 teaspoons vanilla extract

1/2 cup light brown sugar

1 teaspoon ground cinnamon

1/2 teaspoon ground ginger

3-4 bananas, peeled and sliced

2 (4-serving) boxes instant French vanilla or banana pie pudding and pie filling

2 1/2 cups skim milk

1/4 cup crème de banana liqueur, dark rum, or skim milk

1 (8-ounce) container frozen fat-free whipped topping, thawed

1 In 9-inch pie plate or springform pan, combine cookie crumbs, 3 tablespoons melted butter, and vanilla. Press into pie plate. Refrigerate.

2 In nonstick skillet, melt remaining 2 tablespoons butter and add sugar cooking until slightly thickens and bubbly. Add cinnamon, ginger and bananas; cook until bananas are tender. Pour evenly over set crust. Return to refrigerator.

3 In bowl, whisk together pudding, milk and liqueur until thickened. Carefully spread over banana mixture. Top with whipped topping. Refrigerate.

Bananas Foster Pudding Pie (pg 44)

COMFORT FOOD

Easy Roast (pg 155) **or**
Smothered Chicken (pg 23)
Green Bean Casserole (pg 47)

Creamy Mac & Cheese (pg 48)
Best Biscuits (pg 48)
Slice & Bake Chocolate Chip Cookies (pg 49)

Easy Roast

Best Biscuits

Green Bean Casserole

Creamy Mac & Cheese

Slice & Bake Chocolate
Chip Cookies

Smothered Chicken

EASY ROAST

Great recipe for your first roast.
See page 155

SMOTHERED CHICKEN

Who doesn't enjoy chicken and gravy?
See page 23

GREEN BEAN CASSEROLE

This old-fashioned green bean casserole gets an update withstanding the test of time.

Makes 8 (1/2-cup) servings

1/2 cup finely chopped onion

1/2 pound sliced mushrooms

1/2 teaspoon minced garlic

1/4 cup all-purpose flour

2 cups skim milk

1/4 cup nonfat sour cream

Salt and pepper to taste

1 (16-ounce) package frozen French cut green beans

1/2 cup bread crumbs

1 Preheat oven 425°F. Coat 2-quart baking dish with nonstick cooking spray.

2 In large nonstick pot, sauté onion, mushrooms, and garlic 3–5 minutes or until tender. Add flour, stirring, and cook 1 minute. Gradually add milk, whisking constantly.

3 Bring to boil, reduce heat, and cook, stirring until thickened. Remove from heat. Whisk in sour cream and season to taste. Add green beans and mix well.

4 Transfer to prepared dish and sprinkle with bread crumbs. Bake 15–20 minutes or until bubbly.

 D

NUTRITIONAL INFO:

Calories 97

Calories from Fat 5%

Fat 1g

Saturated Fat 0g

Cholesterol 2mg

Sodium 148mg

Carbohydrates 17g

Dietary Fiber 2g

Total Sugars 6g

Protein 6g

Dietary Exchanges:
1 vegetable, 1 starch

TERRIFIC TIP

Any type of green beans may be used — frozen or canned.

CREAMY MAC & CHEESE

Even better and creamier than out of the box.

Makes 6 (2/3-cup) servings

8 ounces small macaroni

2 tablespoons butter

2 tablespoons all-purpose flour

2 cups evaporated fat-free milk or skim milk

4 ounces reduced-fat processed cheese spread

1/4 cup shredded reduced-fat Cheddar cheese

1/4 teaspoon ground mustard, optional

1 Cook macaroni according to package directions. Drain well and set aside.

2 In large pot, melt butter and stir in flour, cooking one minute. Gradually add milk stirring or whisking until combined. Bring to boil, stirring, until mixture slightly thickens.

3 Reduce heat and add cheese spread, Cheddar cheese, ground mustard and season to taste. Cook, stirring, over low heat until cheese is melted. Add macaroni; mixing well.

NUTRITIONAL INFO:

Calories 304

Calories from Fat 22%

Fat 7g

Saturated Fat 4g

Cholesterol 24mg

Sodium 462mg

Carbohydrates 42g

Dietary Fiber 1g

Total Sugars 12g

Protein 17g

Dietary Exchanges:
2 starch, 1 fat free milk, 1 lean meat

BEST BISCUITS

Light, soft interior make these irresistible, especially hot out of the oven. Serve for breakfast, with a soup or whenever.

Makes 9 biscuits

2 cups biscuit baking mix plus extra for patting dough

1/2 cup nonfat plain Greek yogurt or sour cream

1/2 cup lemon lime drink

2 tablespoons butter, melted

1 Preheat oven 450°F. Coat 9x9x2-inch baking pan with nonstick cooking spray.

2 In bowl, combine biscuit mix, yogurt and lemon lime drink until just mixed (soft dough).

3 Sprinkle additional biscuit mix on waxed paper and pat dough out to 1/2-inch thick. Cut with glass or cookie cutter and place in prepared pan. Drizzle with melted butter. Bake 12-15 minutes or until golden brown.

NUTRITIONAL INFO:

Calories 142

Calories from Fat 37%

Fat 6g

Saturated Fat 3g

Cholesterol 7mg

Sodium 358mg

Carbohydrates 19g

Dietary Fiber 1g

Total Sugars 3g

Protein 3g

Dietary Exchanges:
1 1/2 starch, 1 fat

SLICE & BAKE CHOCOLATE CHIP COOKIES

Nothing beats freshly baked hot cookies, so now you can have them whenever you want. Make the dough and refrigerate to bake at your convenience.

Makes 36 cookies

6 tablespoons butter

1/2 cup confectioners' sugar

1/2 cup light brown sugar

2 teaspoons vanilla extract

1 egg

2 cups all-purpose flour

1 teaspoon baking soda

2/3 cup semisweet chocolate chips

1/2 cup chopped pecans

NUTRITIONAL INFO:

Calories 94

Calories from Fat 41%

Fat 4g

Saturated Fat 2g

Cholesterol 10mg

Sodium 55mg

Carbohydrates 13g

Dietary Fiber 1g

Total Sugars 7g

Protein 1g

Dietary Exchanges:
1 other carbohydrate,
1 fat

1 In mixing bowl, beat butter, confectioners' sugar, and brown sugar until combined. Add vanilla and egg beating until creamy.

2 In small bowl, combine flour and baking soda. Add to sugar mixture and beat until well mixed. Stir in chocolate chips and pecans.

3 Mold dough into two 12-inch logs and wrap in plastic wrap in refrigerator 1 hour.

4 When ready to bake preheat oven 350°F. Coat baking sheet with nonstick cooking spray. Cut dough into about 1/2-inch slices and place on prepared pan. Bake 8-10 minutes or until done.

SPORTS SPREAD

Spinach Dip (pg 57)
Cheesy Burger Dip (pg 132) or
Taco Dip (pg 19)
Parmesan Pita Pick-Ups (pg 131)

All American Potato Skins (pg 52)
Ham & Cheese Sliders (pg 53) or
Beef Sliders (pg 156)
Ooey Gooey Squares (pg 54)

All American Potato Skins

Ham & Cheese Sliders

Taco Dip

Spinach Dip

Parmesan Pita Pick-Ups

Ooey Gooey Squares

Cheesy Burger Dip

Beef Sliders

SPINACH DIP

Serve this fantastically flavored cold spinach dip in different ways — with veggies, pitas, chips, sandwiches or stuff cucumber and celery.

Makes 24 (2-tablespoon) servings

1 (10-ounce) package frozen chopped spinach

1 (8-ounce) package reduced-fat cream cheese

3/4 cup Greek nonfat plain yogurt

2 tablespoons lemon juice

1/2 cup chopped green onions

2 tablespoons chopped parsley

1/2 teaspoon dried dill weed leaves

1/2 teaspoon seasoned salt or season to taste

1/4 cup reduced-fat feta cheese

1 Thaw, squeeze and drain chopped spinach. In bowl combine all ingredients except feta, mixing well. Stir in feta and refrigerate until serving.

 D

NUTRITIONAL INFO:
Calories 35
Calories from Fat 58%
Fat 2g
Saturated Fat 1g
Cholesterol 7mg
Sodium 105mg
Carbohydrates 1g
Dietary Fiber 0g
Total Sugars 1g
Protein 2g
Dietary Exchanges:
1/2 fat

CHEESY BURGER DIP

My two favorites, ground meat and cheese in a dip.
See page 132

TACO DIP

A taco-style layered hot dip.
See page 19

PARMESAN PITA PICK-UPS

Crispy Italian seasoned pita chips.
See page 131

ALL AMERICAN POTATO SKINS
with HORSERADISH SAUCE

 ❄ **D**

NUTRITIONAL INFO:

Calories 62

Calories from Fat 22%

Fat 2g

Saturated Fat 1g

Cholesterol 7mg

Sodium 96mg

Carbohydrates 9g

Dietary Fiber 1g

Total Sugars 1g

Protein 4g

Dietary Exchanges:
1/2 starch,
1/2 lean meat

TERRIFIC TIP

*Use extra potato
pulp to make
mashed potatoes
for tomorrow's
dinner.*

An all-time popular restaurant pick-up that you can easily make yourself and a guaranteed winner, especially at any sports viewing party.

Makes 12 potato skins

6 medium baking potatoes

Garlic powder

4 slices turkey bacon, cooked and crumbled

1/2 cup chopped tomatoes

1/2 cup chopped green onions

2/3 cup reduced-fat shredded Cheddar cheese

1/2 cup fat-free plain yogurt

1 tablespoon horseradish

1 Pierce potatoes all over with fork. Microwave 8-10 minutes depending on size (or bake 425°F. for 50 minutes). When potatoes are cool enough to handle, cut in half lengthwise; scoop out pulp, leaving a 1/4-inch shell (save pulp for another use). Cut potato skins in half. Sprinkle with garlic powder.

2 Place potatoes skins on a baking sheet lined with foil. Coat skins with nonstick cooking spray.

3 Bake 475°F. for 5-7 minutes; turn and coat skins' other side with nonstick cooking spray. Bake until crisp, about 5-7 minutes more.

4 In small bowl, mix together bacon, tomatoes, green onions, and cheese. Sprinkle mixture inside skins. Bake 2 minutes longer or until the cheese is melted.

5 Meanwhile, in small bowl mix together yogurt and horseradish. Serve with potato skins.

HAM & CHEESE SLIDERS

Who said ham and cheese sandwiches are boring? Try this fantastic slider and it will be a party or snack favorite!

Makes 24 sliders

24 miniature rolls

1/3 cup Dijon mustard

1/2 pound thinly sliced lean ham, cut into small pieces

2 cups shredded Jarlsberg cheese (light Swiss)

Poppy Seed Sauce (see recipe)

1 Preheat oven 350°F. Line baking sheet with foil.

2 Split rolls in half, lay on prepared pan. Spread each bottom half with mustard and layer ham and cheese. Replace tops. Place filled rolls close together on baking sheet. Drizzle Poppy Seed Sauce (recipe follows) evenly over sliders.

3 Cover with foil and bake 12-15 minutes or until cheese is melted. Remove cover and bake 2 minutes longer.

POPPY SEED SAUCE

1 tablespoon poppy seeds

4 tablespoons butter, melted

2 tablespoons finely chopped onion

Hot sauce to taste

1 In small bowl, mix together all ingredients.

NUTRITIONAL INFO:

Calories 148

Calories from Fat 36%

Fat 6g

Saturated Fat 3g

Cholesterol 24mg

Sodium 324mg

Carbohydrates 16g

Dietary Fiber 1g

Total Sugars 4g

Protein 8g

Dietary Exchanges:
1 starch, 1 lean meat, 1/2 fat

TERRIFIC TIP

If making ahead, keep in refrigerator or freezer and add poppy seed sauce when ready to bake.

BEEF SLIDERS

Turn leftover meat into this scrumptious slider.

See page 156

OOEY GOOEY SQUARES

This recipe has probably been my most requested and all-time favorite bar cookie for all ages. Best of all, it's so easy and quick.

Makes 48 squares

1 (18.25-ounce) box yellow cake mix

1/2 cup butter, melted

1 egg

1 tablespoon water

1 (8-ounce) package reduced-fat cream cheese

1 (16-ounce) box confectioners' sugar

2 egg whites

1 teaspoon vanilla extract

1 cup semisweet chocolate chips

1. Preheat oven to 350° F. Coat 13x9x2-inch baking pan with nonstick cooking spray.

2. In mixing bowl, beat together cake mix, butter, egg, and water until well mixed. Spread batter into prepared pan.

3. In mixing bowl, beat together cream cheese, confectioners' sugar, egg whites, and vanilla. Stir in chocolate chips. Pour this mixture over batter in pan.

4. Bake 40-50 minutes or until top is golden brown. Cool to room temperature and cut into squares.

NUTRITIONAL INFO:

Calories 138

Calories from Fat 36%

Fat 6g

Saturated Fat 3g

Cholesterol 13mg

Sodium 112mg

Carbohydrates 21g

Dietary Fiber 0g

Total Sugars 17g

Protein 2g

Dietary Exchanges:
1 1/2 other
carbohydrate,
1 fat

TERRIFIC TIP

I always keep these pantry-friendly ingredients for when I need a fast emergency dessert.

FANCY FOOD

Seared Tuna with Avocado Salsa
on Rice Crackers (pg 56)

Marinated Shrimp & Artichokes (pg 57)

Candied Pecan Brie (pg 57)

Crabmeat Brie Dip (pg 58)

Italian Layered Spread (pg 59)

Mini Heavenly Cheesecake Bites
with Caramel Topping (pg 60)

Candied Pecan Brie

Seared Tuna with Avocado
Salsa on Rice Crackers

Mini Heavenly Cheesecake Bites
with Caramel Topping

Crabmeat Brie Dip

Marinated Shrimp & Artichokes

Italian Layered Spread

SEARED TUNA *with* AVOCADO SALSA *on* RICE CRACKER

D

NUTRITIONAL INFO:

Calories 135

Calories from Fat 31%

Fat 5g

Saturated Fat 1g

Cholesterol 11mg

Sodium 182mg

Carbohydrates 15g

Dietary Fiber 2g

Total Sugars 6g

Protein 8g

Dietary Exchanges:
1/2 starch, 1 vegetable,
1 lean meat

TERRIFIC TIP

Sweetened chili sauce is usually found jarred in the Asian section of the grocery store.

Rice crackers are the perfect tasting cracker for this recipe.

This amazing blend of flavors easily comes together by preparing avocado salsa and searing tuna ahead of time. Just assemble when ready to serve.

Makes about 12 (4-cracker) servings

1 (12-ounce) about 1/2-inch thick tuna fillet

Pepper and salt to taste

1 tablespoon olive oil

1 1/2 cups finely chopped avocados

1 cup finely chopped tomatoes

1/2 cup finely chopped red onion

3 tablespoons lime juice

48 rice crackers

1/2 cup sweetened chili sauce

1. Season tuna heavily with pepper and salt to taste. In nonstick skillet, over medium-high heat, heat oil and sear tuna quickly on each side (sushi-rare tuna in middle). Cool. Slice tuna against grain into 48 small squares.

2. In bowl, combine avocados, tomatoes, red onion, and lime juice. Season to taste.

3. To assemble: place small amount of avocado salsa on rice cracker, top with tuna slice, and drizzle with chili sauce.

MARINATED SHRIMP & ARTICHOKES

Always popular — use as a dip or enjoy leftovers as a salad.

Makes 32 (1/4-cup) servings

1/4 cup seasoned rice vinegar

3 tablespoons olive oil

1 (0.75-oz.) envelope zesty Italian dressing mix

1 pound peeled medium shrimp, cooked

1/2 cup chopped green onions

1 (14-ounce) can artichoke hearts, drained and quartered

1/3 cup Kalamata olives, sliced or halved

1 cup grape tomato halves

1/3 cup crumbled feta cheese, optional

1 In small bowl, whisk together vinegar, olive oil, and dressing mix. In large bowl, combine all remaining ingredients and toss with vinaigrette. Cover and refrigerate 8-24 hours, time permitting.

D

NUTRITIONAL INFO:
Calories 38
Calories from Fat 46%
Fat 2g
Saturated Fat 0g
Cholesterol 25mg
Sodium 226mg
Carbohydrates 2g
Dietary Fiber 0g
Total Sugars 1g
Protein 3g
Dietary Exchanges:
1/2 lean meat

CANDIED PECAN BRIE

Easy showpiece recipe — ready in minutes.

Makes 8 (1-ounce) servings

1 (8-ounce) round Brie cheese

1/4 cup pecans halves

2 tablespoons light brown sugar

1/2 teaspoon ground cinnamon

1 tablespoon maple syrup

1/2 teaspoon vanilla extract

1 Preheat oven 325ºF.

2 Remove top rind of Brie. Place Brie in shallow baking dish.

3 In small skillet coated with nonstick cooking spray, cook pecans, stirring about 2 minutes or until golden brown. Add brown sugar, cinnamon, maple syrup, and vanilla stirring, until brown sugar is melted and combined. Watch carefully, as cooks quickly. Top Brie with pecan mixture.

4 Bake 8-10 minutes, or until Brie is soft. Let sit 5 minutes before serving (may heat in microwave).

NUTRITIONAL INFO:
Calories 139
Calories from Fat 66%
Fat 10g
Saturated Fat 5g
Cholesterol 28mg
Sodium 180mg
Carbohydrates 6g
Dietary Fiber 0g
Total Sugars 5g
Protein 6g
Dietary Exchanges:
1/2 other carbohydrate, 1 lean meat, 1 1/2 fat

CRABMEAT BRIE DIP

Splurge with this divine, creamy, and rich tasting crab dip, taking minutes to make. Best with fresh crabmeat but canned may be used.

Makes 24 (1/4-cup) servings

1 teaspoon minced garlic

1/2 cup chopped onion

3 cups baby spinach, packed

1 cup shredded part-skim mozzarella cheese

1/2 cup nonfat plain Greek yogurt

1 (8-ounce) package reduced-fat cream cheese

1 tablespoon lemon juice

1/4 teaspoon cayenne pepper (or to taste)

6 ounces Brie cheese, rind removed and cut into cubes

1 pound lump crabmeat, picked for shells

1/2 cup chopped green onions

1 In nonstick pot coated with nonstick cooking spray, sauté garlic, onion, and spinach about 5 minutes until tender. Add remaining ingredients except crabmeat and green onions.

2 Cook over low heat, stirring, until cheese is melted and mixture creamy. Carefully stir in crabmeat and green onions.

NUTRITIONAL INFO:

Calories 86

Calories from Fat 53%

Fat 5g

Saturated Fat 3g

Cholesterol 31mg

Sodium 191mg

Carbohydrates 1g

Dietary Fiber 0g

Total Sugars 1g

Protein 8g

Dietary Exchanges:
1 lean meat, 1/2 fat

TERRIFIC TIP

If using fresh crabmeat in slow cooker, fold in before serving.

Great way to serve: keeping warm in slow cooker.

ITALIAN LAYERED SPREAD

Open jars and layer ingredients for an impressive appetizer. Make ahead, refrigerate and be the most admired cook.

Makes 16-20 servings

2 (8-ounce) packages reduced-fat cream cheese

1/3 cup crumbled reduced-fat feta cheese

1 tablespoon dried Italian seasoning

1/4 cup shredded parmesan cheese

1 cup olive salad mix, well drained, divided

1/2 cup roasted red peppers, well drained and chopped

1 (6-ounce) jar marinated artichokes, well drained and chopped

1/4 cup chopped green onions

1. In bowl, mix together cream cheese, feta, and Italian seasoning until smooth. Line an 8x5x2-inch loaf pan with plastic wrap, with enough plastic wrap to go over sizes to fold over finished recipe.

2. Layer ingredients beginning with all the Parmesan cheese, 1/2 cup olive salad mix, 1 cup cream cheese mixture, all the roasted red peppers, all the artichokes, remaining 1/2 cup olive salad mix, all the green onions, and remaining 1/2 cup cream cheese mixture.

3. Fold plastic wrap over top and compress gently. Refrigerate at least several hours before serving. To serve, pull plastic wrap from top, invert on serving plate and easily remove plastic wrap.

NUTRITIONAL INFO:
Calories 103
Calories from Fat 77%
Fat 9g
Saturated Fat 3g
Cholesterol 19mg
Sodium 344mg
Carbohydrates 3g
Dietary Fiber 0g
Total Sugars 1g
Protein 3g
Dietary Exchanges:
2 fat

TERRIFIC TIP

By covering the pan with plastic wrap, when you invert the spread, it easily comes out perfect every time.

Can't find olive salad, raid olive bar at grocery. Finely chop and make your own.

MINI HEAVENLY CHEESECAKE BITES
with CRUNCHY TOPPING

A bite of decadence with a creamy filling and a crunchy topping laced with caramel sauce.

Makes 18-20 bites

1/2 (15-ounce) package refrigerated pie crusts

4 ounces reduced-fat cream cheese

1/4 cup confectioners' sugar

1 teaspoon vanilla extract

1/4 (8-ounce) container frozen fat-free whipped topping, thawed

3 tablespoons flaked coconut

1/4 cup chopped pecans

3 tablespoons caramel topping

1. Preheat oven 425°F.

2. Unroll pie crust on wax paper and use 2-inch round cutter or glass, to make about 18 rounds. Press rounds into ungreased miniature muffin tins, pressing to make a cup. Bake 8-10 minutes until light brown. Cool completely. Remove from tins.

3. In mixing bowl, beat cream cheese, sugar, and vanilla until creamy. Fold in whipped topping. Fill miniature shells with cream cheese filling. Refrigerate.

4. Reduce oven 350°F. Place coconut and pecans on baking sheet and bake 7-9 minutes or until toasted. Cool. When ready to serve, sprinkle each tart with coconut pecan mixture and drizzle with a touch of caramel sauce.

NUTRITIONAL INFO:

Calories 88

Calories from Fat 50%

Fat 5g

Saturated Fat 2g

Cholesterol 5mg

Sodium 86mg

Carbohydrates 10g

Dietary Fiber 0g

Total Sugars 4g

Protein 1g

Dietary Exchanges:
1/2 other carbohydrate,
1 fat

TERRIFIC TIP

Save a step by using frozen miniature phyllo pastry shells, thawed and cooked at 350°F. 3-5 minutes. Cool and fill.

SUMMER SENSATIONS

Shrimp Salad with Asian Vinaigrette (pg 62)
Cucumber, Mint & Feta Salad (pg 63)
Strawberry Cheesecake Parfaits (pg 174)

Shrimp Salad with Asian Vinaigrette

Cucumber, Mint & Feta Salad

Strawberry Cheesecake Parfaits

SHRIMP SALAD *with* ASIAN VINAIGRETTE

This salad came about as I had leftover grilled Asian shrimp and corn on the cob so I created a fantastic Asian Vinaigrette and turned my leftovers into an awesome salad!

Makes 4-6 servings

1 1/2 pounds medium peeled cooked shrimp, or use Asian Shrimp recipe (pg 143)

3 cups shredded red cabbage

6 cups baby spinach (9-ounce bag)

1 red bell pepper, cut into strips

1/2 cup corn (frozen or leftover corn on the cob)

1 bunch green onions, chopped

1 (3-ounce) package Ramen noodles, broken up, with seasoning packet discarded

1/2 cup sliced almonds

Asian Vinaigrette (recipe follows)

1. In large bowl, combine all ingredients except Ramen noodles and almonds; set aside.

2. Preheat oven 350°F. Spread Ramen noodles and almonds on baking sheet and bake about 10 minutes or until light brown. Cool.

3. To serve, add noodles and almonds, toss with Asian Vinaigrette (see recipe).

ASIAN VINAIGRETTE

1/4 cup seasoned rice vinegar

2 teaspoons low-sodium soy sauce

1/2 teaspoon Dijon mustard

1/2 teaspoon minced garlic

1/2 teaspoon ground ginger

1/8 teaspoon red pepper flakes

2 tablespoons olive oil

1. In small bowl, whisk together all ingredients except oil. Gradually add oil, whisking constantly, until well combined.

NUTRITIONAL INFO:

Calories 282

Calories from Fat 41%

Fat 13g

Saturated Fat 3g

Cholesterol 143mg

Sodium 515mg

Carbohydrates 23g

Dietary Fiber 5g

Total Sugars 7g

Protein 21g

Dietary Exchanges:
1 starch,
2 vegetable, 3 lean meat, 1/2 fat

TERRIFIC TIP

For a time-saver, if recipe calls for toasted almonds, look for them already toasted in the grocery.

Transfer to an airtight container, refrigerate and use within a week.

CUCUMBER, MINT & FETA SALAD

Turn cucumbers into this refreshing flavor combination.

 D

Makes 4 (3/4-cup) servings

3 cups thinly sliced peeled cucumber

1/4 cup crumbled reduced-fat feta

1/4 cup seasoned rice vinegar

1 tablespoon olive oil

3 tablespoons chopped green onions

3 tablespoons fresh chopped mint

2 tablespoons pine nuts, toasted

Salt and pepper to taste

1 In bowl, combine cucumber and feta.

2 In small bowl, whisk together vinegar, oil and green onions. Toss with cucumber and feta. Add mint and pine nuts. Season to taste.

NUTRITIONAL INFO:
Calories 96
Calories from Fat 57%
Fat 6g
Saturated Fat 1g
Cholesterol 3mg
Sodium 320mg
Carbohydrates 7g
Dietary Fiber 1g
Total Sugars 6g
Protein 3g
Dietary Exchanges:
1/2 other carbohydrate, 1 fat

This is one time fresh mint makes a difference. Pine nuts are pricey so if you don't want to use them, just leave them out.

STRAWBERRY CHEESECAKE PARFAITS

Attention cheesecake fan — berries and cheesecake make a dynamite combination!

See page 174

BEST BASIC BARBECUE

Brisket with Mango Barbecue Sauce

Sweet Potato Cornbread

Cool Coleslaw

Baked Beans

S'Mores Cookies

COOL COLESLAW

Makes 10 (1/2-cup) servings

 D

4 cups shredded cabbage (bag coleslaw)

1 bunch green onions, chopped

1/2 cup chopped red onion

1/2 cup chopped cucumber

2 tablespoons lime juice

2 tablespoons cider or seasoned rice vinegar

1 tablespoon olive oil

1 (11-ounce) can mandarin oranges, drained

2 tablespoons chopped fresh mint

1/4 cup coarsely chopped peanuts

NUTRITIONAL INFO:
Calories 65
Calories from Fat 41%
Fat 3g
Saturated Fat 0g
Cholesterol 0mg
Sodium 51mg
Carbohydrates 8g
Dietary Fiber 2g
Total Sugars 5g
Protein 2g
Dietary Exchanges:
1/2 other carbohydrate,
1/2 fat

1. In large bowl, combine cabbage, green onions, red onion, and cucumber. In small bowl, whisk together lime juice, vinegar and oil; pour over slaw and mix.

2. Carefully add mandarin oranges. To serve, add mint and peanuts, mixing well. Season to taste.

SWEET POTATO CORNBREAD

Fresh or canned sweet potatoes may be used.

  D

Makes 12 squares

1 (6-ounce) package yellow cornbread mix

2 tablespoons sugar

1/2 teaspoon ground cinnamon

2/3 cup skim milk

1 egg, beaten

1/2 cup cooked mashed Louisiana yams (sweet potatoes)

NUTRITIONAL INFO:
Calories 84
Calories from Fat 19%
Fat 2g
Saturated Fat 0g
Cholesterol 16mg
Sodium 244mg
Carbohydrates 15g
Dietary Fiber 0g
Total Sugars 5g
Protein 2g
Dietary Exchanges:
1 starch

1. Preheat oven 400°F. Coat 8x8x2-inch pan coated with nonstick cooking spray.

2. In bowl, combine cornbread mix, sugar, and cinnamon. Stir in remaining ingredients, mixing until moistened; don't over mix.

3. Transfer batter into prepared pan. Bake 20 minutes or until top is golden brown.

BRISKET *with* MANGO BARBECUE SAUCE

Finger-lickin' best brisket with a surprisingly few amount of ingredients. Serve with this irresistible Mango Barbecue Sauce as an entrée, sandwich or make brisket quesadillas for a knock-out recipe.

Makes 10 (4-ounce) servings

NUTRITIONAL INFO:
Calories 259
Calories from Fat 37%
Fat 10g
Saturated Fat 4g
Cholesterol 95mg
Sodium 243mg
Carbohydrates 9g
Dietary Fiber 1g
Total Sugars 7g
Protein 31g
Dietary Exchanges:
1/2 other
carbohydrate,
4 lean meat

3 pound brisket, trimmed

1 tablespoon chili powder

2 teaspoons garlic powder

Pepper to taste

1 (12-ounce) can diet Dr. Pepper

Mango Barbecue Sauce (recipe follows)

1 Preheat oven 300°F.

2 Season brisket with chili powder, garlic powder and pepper. Place in roaster or large pot. Pour Dr. Pepper over top. Bake, covered, 5 hours or until tender. Serve with Mango Barbecue Sauce (see recipe).

MANGO BARBECUE SAUCE

Keep in the refrigerator to serve with any grilled meat.

1 onion, finely chopped

1/2 cup ketchup

2 tablespoons lemon juice

1 tablespoon Worcestershire sauce

1/3 cup mango chutney

1 In small pot coated with nonstick cooking spray, sauté onion until tender. Add remaining ingredients, cooking over low heat 10 minutes.

Cook in crock pot on low 8 hours.

Serving Option: Brisket Quesadillas: Lay out tortillas and cover with shredded brisket, 1-2 tablespoons Mango Barbecue Sauce, Brie and red onions. Top with another tortilla. Cook in heated skillet until bottom is crisp, flip over, and cook another 1-2 minutes. Cut into fourths.

BAKED BEANS

A different twist to a traditional dish — a remarkable recipe!

Makes 16 (1/2-cup) servings

4 slices center cut or turkey bacon, chopped

1 onion, chopped

1 1/2 teaspoons minced garlic

1 cup light beer

1 (15 1/2-ounce) can tomato sauce

1/4 cup light brown sugar

2 tablespoons balsamic vinegar

2 tablespoons molasses, optional

1 tablespoon Dijon mustard

3 (15 1/2-ounce) cans cannellini or great Northern beans, rinsed and drained

NUTRITIONAL INFO:
Calories 100
Calories from Fat 8%
Fat 1g
Saturated Fat 0g
Cholesterol 2mg
Sodium 372mg
Carbohydrates 18g
Dietary Fiber 3g
Total Sugars 5g
Protein 4g
Dietary Exchanges:
1 starch

1. Preheat oven 350°F. Coat 2-quart baking dish with nonstick cooking spray.

2. In large nonstick pot, cook bacon until crispy. Add onion and garlic; cook until tender, 5-7 minutes. Add remaining ingredients except beans. Bring to boil, reduce heat, and cook 5 minutes.

3. Add beans, stirring to mix well. Transfer to baking dish and bake, covered, 35-40 minutes.

TERRIFIC TIP

Can make earlier and bake when ready to serve.

S'MORES COOKIES

Melt in your mouth cookies.
See page 181

MEATLESS MONDAY

Corn Dip (pg 69)
Black Bean Soup (pg 70)
Roasted Tomato & Brie Pasta (pg 71)

Artichoke Bread (pg 72)
No-Bake German Chocolate Mounds (pg 184)

Corn Dip

Artichoke Bread

Black Bean Soup

No-Bake German Chocolate Mounds

Roasted Tomato & Brie Pasta

CORN DIP

A quick and easy, economical dip that's creamy, crunchy, and spicy in each bite.

 D

Makes 10 (1/4-cup) servings

1 tablespoon olive oil

2 cups frozen corn, thawed

1/2 cup chopped onion

1/3 cup chopped red bell pepper

1/2 cup chopped green onions

2 tablespoons chopped jalapeño (found in jar)

2 tablespoons light mayonnaise

1/3 cup nonfat sour cream

2/3 cup shredded reduced-fat sharp Cheddar cheese

Salt and pepper to taste

1 In large nonstick skillet, heat oil and add corn cooking over medium heat, stirring until golden brown, about 5 minutes.

2 Add onion and pepper, sauté until tender, 3-4 minutes.

3 Add green onions, jalapeño, mayonnaise, sour cream and cheese, stirring until heated and bubbly; cheese is melted. Season to taste.

NUTRITIONAL INFO:

Calories 89

Calories from Fat 39%

Fat 4g

Saturated Fat 1g

Cholesterol 7mg

Sodium 108mg

Carbohydrates 11g

Dietary Fiber 1g

Total Sugars 3g

Protein 4g

Dietary Exchanges:
1/2 starch, 1 fat

TERRIFIC TIP

If making ahead of time, refrigerate and reheat in microwave until heated.

BLACK BEAN SOUP

Canned black beans turn a time consuming recipe into a tasty simple vegetarian soup.

Makes 5 (1-cup) servings

1/2 cup chopped onion

1/2 cup chopped green bell pepper

1 teaspoon minced garlic

1 (14 1/2-ounce) can chopped tomatoes with juice

1 (10-ounce) can chopped tomatoes and green chilies

1 (4-ounce) can chopped green chilies

1/2 teaspoon ground cumin

1/2 teaspoon chili powder

1 (15-ounce) can black beans, rinsed and drained

1 (14-1/2-ounce) can vegetable broth

Salt and pepper to taste

1. In nonstick pot coated with nonstick cooking spray, sauté onion, green pepper, and garlic until tender, 7 minutes.

2. Add remaining ingredients to pot, heating well. Remove 2 cups black bean soup, puree in food processor or blender until smooth.

3. Return pureed mixture to pot, bring to boil. Lower heat, simmer 10 minutes. Season to taste.

NUTRITIONAL INFO:

Calories 116

Calories from Fat 6%

Fat 1g

Saturated Fat 0g

Cholesterol 0mg

Sodium 1012mg

Carbohydrates 13g

Dietary Fiber 21g

Total Sugars 4g

Protein 6g

Dietary Exchanges:
1 starch, 1 vegetable, 1/2 lean meat

TERRIFIC TIP

Try serving with dollop of nonfat sour cream and reduced-fat Cheddar cheese.

Use low-sodium chicken broth or water to reduce sodium for diabetic friendly recipe.

ROASTED TOMATO & BRIE PASTA

Roasted tomatoes combined with mild creamy Brie and crunchy almonds create an unbeatable pasta dish. Take a short-cut with canned fired-roasted tomatoes and dried basil or try roasting tomatoes and fresh basil, either way, you have a winner!

Makes 6 (1-cup) servings

12 ounces spiral pasta

3 tablespoons olive oil

1 (14 1/2-ounce) can diced fire-roasted tomatoes or roasted tomatoes (see recipe)

2 teaspoons dried basil leaves or 1/4 cup loosely packed fresh basil, chopped

1 teaspoon minced garlic

1/2 cup cubed Brie, rind removed

1/4 cup sliced almonds, toasted

Salt and pepper to taste

1. Cook pasta according to package directions: drain.

2. In large nonstick skillet, heat oil and add tomatoes, basil and garlic to skillet. Add Brie, stirring until just begins to melt.

3. Transfer Brie mixture to pasta, add almonds and carefully toss together. Season to taste.

ROASTED TOMATOES

3 cups coarsely chopped fresh tomatoes

2 tablespoons olive oil

1 teaspoon dried basil leaves or 1 tablespoon fresh basil

Salt and pepper to taste

1. Preheat oven 425°F. Line baking sheet with foil.

2. On prepared pan, combine tomatoes, oil, basil and season to taste. Roast 25-30 minutes or until done and slightly blackened.

NUTRITIONAL INFO:

Calories 342

Calories from Fat 32%

Fat 12g

Saturated Fat 3g

Cholesterol 9mg

Sodium 220mg

Carbohydrates 47g

Dietary Fiber 3g

Total Sugars 4g

Protein 11g

Dietary Exchanges:
3 starch, 1 vegetable, 2 fat

TERRIFIC TIP

Try using roasted fresh tomatoes for the canned (see recipe). If roasting fresh tomatoes, use 2 tablespoons olive oil in cooking and 1 tablespoon olive oil roasting tomatoes.

ARTICHOKE BREAD

This versatile "melt-in-your-mouth" bread makes a great side, snack or appetizer.

Makes 16 slices

NUTRITIONAL INFO:

Calories 117
Calories from Fat 24%
Fat 3g
Saturated Fat 1g
Cholesterol 8mg
Sodium 285mg
Carbohydrates 17g
Dietary Fiber 1g
Total Sugars 1g
Protein 5g
Dietary Exchanges:
1 starch, 1/2 fat

TERRIFIC TIP

Use a serrated knife to cut bread easier.

1 (14-ounce) can artichoke hearts, drained and chopped

1/2 cup chopped green onions

1/2 teaspoon minced garlic

2 ounces reduced-fat cream cheese

2 tablespoons light mayonnaise

1/3 cup nonfat sour cream

2/3 cup shredded part-skim mozzarella cheese

2 tablespoons grated Parmesan cheese

1 loaf Italian bread

1. Preheat oven 350°F.

2. In bowl, mix together all ingredients except Parmesan cheese and bread.

3. Slice bread in half lengthwise and hollow 1/2-inch out of the center of both halves of bread. Spread artichoke mixture evenly on top of each bread half. Sprinkle each half with Parmesan cheese.

4. Bake, covered with foil, about 20 minutes. Remove foil and continue baking 5-7 minutes or until cheese is melted and golden. Slice and serve.

NO BAKE GERMAN CHOCOLATE MOUNDS

Cure your sweet tooth in a hurry with this yummy treat.

See page 184

MEDITERRANEAN MENU

Artichoke Hummus (pg 18)
Chopped Greek Salad (pg 74)

Pork Pitas (pg 75) **or**
Chicken Schwarma (pg 76)

Chicken Schwarma

Pork Pitas

Chopped Greek Salad

Artichoke Hummus

ARTICHOKE HUMMUS

Artichoke + hummus = fantastic
See page 18

CHOPPED GREEK SALAD

Leftover ingredients made an amazing chopped salad!

Makes 5 (1-cup) servings

2 cups chopped fresh baby spinach

1 cup chopped peeled cucumber

1/2 cup chopped sun-dried tomatoes, reconstituted

1/4 cup chopped red onion

1/4 cup chopped avocado

1/4 cup crumbled reduced-fat feta cheese

2 tablespoons sliced Kalamata olives

1/4 cup chopped pecans, toasted

2 tablespoons lemon juice

1 tablespoon vinegar

1 teaspoon olive oil

Pepper to taste

1. In large bowl, combine all ingredients except lemon juice, vinegar and olive oil. In small bowl, whisk together lemon juice, vinegar and oil. Toss with spinach mixture and season to taste.

D

NUTRITIONAL INFO:
Calories 110
Calories from Fat 60%
Fat 8g
Saturated Fat 1g
Cholesterol 3mg
Sodium 198mg
Carbohydrates 8g
Dietary Fiber 2g
Total Sugars 3g
Protein 3g
Dietary Exchanges:
2 vegetable, 1 1/2 fat

TERRIFIC TIP

Reconstitute sun-dried tomatoes, let stand in hot water 5 minutes, and drain.

Serving Option: Toss in grilled chicken or any leftover meat for an awesome main dish salad.

PORK PITAS

Oregano seasoned pork slices, tomato topping, and a mild creamy dill sauce create a quick Mediterranean taco-style pita.

Makes 4 servings

2 tablespoons red wine vinegar, divided

2 teaspoons dried oregano leaves

2 teaspoons olive oil, divided

1 teaspoon minced garlic

1 pound boneless center-cut loin pork chops, trimmed of fat

3/4 cup plain nonfat plain yogurt or Greek yogurt

2 teaspoons dried dill weed leaves

Salt and pepper to taste

1 1/2 cups chopped tomatoes

1 cup chopped peeled cucumber

1/2 cup chopped red onion

1/4 cup reduced-fat feta cheese

2 pitas, cut in quarters

1. In resealable plastic bag, combine 1 tablespoon vinegar, oregano, 1 teaspoon olive oil and garlic. Add pork and marinate in refrigerator one hour or time permitting.

2. In small bowl, mix together yogurt with dill, remaining 1 tablespoon vinegar, 1 teaspoon olive oil and season to taste. Refrigerate, covered, until ready to use.

3. In small bowl, combine tomatoes, cucumber, onion, and feta if desired. Season to taste.

4. Heat a nonstick grill pan coated with nonstick cooking spray and cook pork (discard marinade) over medium-high heat until browned and done, 4-5 minutes each side. Slice.

5. Stuff sliced pork with tomato and yogurt mixture into pitas.

D

NUTRITIONAL INFO:

Calories 299

Calories from Fat 27%

Fat 9g

Saturated Fat 2g

Cholesterol 67mg

Sodium 247mg

Carbohydrates 26g

Dietary Fiber 2g

Total Sugars 7g

Protein 28g

Dietary Exchanges:
1 1/2 starch,
1 vegetable,
3 lean meat

TERRIFIC TIP

Leftover grilled pork tenderloins are another great option.

Also great with flour tortillas.

CHICKEN SCHWARMA

The secret is in the marinade, a savory spice mixture, that infuses the chicken with fantastic flavor making this an easy home version of a familiar favorite. (The long ingredient list is for the marinade.)

Makes 6 pitas

D

NUTRITIONAL INFO:
Calories 376
Calories from Fat 14%
Fat 6g
Saturated Fat 1g
Cholesterol 97mg
Sodium 513mg
Carbohydrates 40g
Dietary Fiber 6g
Total Sugars 5g
Protein 42g
Dietary Exchanges:
2 1/2 starch,
1 vegetable,
4 1/2 lean meat

1/2 cup nonfat plain Greek yogurt

2 tablespoons lemon juice

1 tablespoon minced garlic

1/2 teaspoon dried oregano leaves

1/2 teaspoon ground cumin

1/2 teaspoon ground cinnamon

1/4 teaspoon ground cloves, optional

2 pounds boneless, skinless chicken breasts

Yogurt Sauce, (recipe follows)

6 whole wheat pitas

1 cucumber, peeled and thinly sliced

4 Roma tomatoes, thinly sliced

1 small red onion, thinly sliced

Romaine lettuce

1 In shallow dish or large plastic bag, combine yogurt, lemon juice, garlic, oregano, cumin, cinnamon and cloves, if desired, mixing well. Add chicken to marinade, coat well, and refrigerate 4-24 hours, time permitted.

2 In large nonstick skillet, cook chicken or grill until done, about 15-20 minutes, turning halfway through. When done, thinly slice.

3 To make pitas, spread Yogurt Sauce (see recipe) on pita, top with chicken, cucumber, tomatoes, onion and lettuce. Roll sandwich closed (wrap sandwich in foil to help stay closed).

YOGURT SAUCE

1/2 cup nonfat plain Greek Yogurt

1/4 teaspoon minced garlic

1/4 teaspoon dried dill weed leaves

Salt to taste

1 In small bowl, mix together all ingredients. Refrigerate.

ITALIAN FEAST

Calzones

Chocolate Italian Cream Cake

Caprese Salad

CALZONES

NUTRITIONAL INFO:
Calories 190
Calories from Fat 23%
Fat 5g
Saturated Fat 1g
Cholesterol 20mg
Sodium 433mg
Carbohydrates 24g
Dietary Fiber 2g
Total Sugars 5g
Protein 12g
Dietary Exchanges:
1 starch, 1 vegetable,
1 lean meat

TERRIFIC TIP

Be creative and add your favorite vegetables to the calzone filling.

My calzones might not look picture perfect but when it comes to taste, this easy-to-make scrumptious recipe gets a thumbs up!

Makes 8 calzones

1/2 pound ground sirloin

1/2 cup chopped onion

1 cup sliced mushrooms

1 teaspoon minced garlic

1 teaspoon dried basil leaves

1/2 teaspoon dried oregano leaves

Salt and pepper to taste

1 (10-13.8-ounce) can refrigerated pizza crust

1/2 cup shredded part-skim mozzarella cheese

1 cup marinara sauce

1 Preheat oven 425°F. Coat baking sheet with nonstick cooking spray.

2 In large nonstick skillet, cook meat, onion, mushrooms and garlic until meat is done; drain excess fat. Add basil, oregano and season to taste. Set aside.

3 Unroll dough; pat and stretch into rectangle on floured surface. Cut dough into eight squares. Spoon about 1/4 cup meat mixture on each square. Sprinkle evenly with cheese.

4 Fold dough over filling forming into a semi-circle mashing edges to form rim. Press fork along edges to seal dough. Prick tops of calzones with fork to allow steam to escape. Place on baking sheet.

5 Bake 10-12 minutes or until lightly browned. Serve with marinara sauce.

CAPRESE SALAD

Ripe juicy tomatoes, fresh mozzarella and basil, this salad rocks!

Makes 4 (2/3-cup) serving

2 cups sliced tomatoes or Roma tomatoes

3 ounces fresh mozzarella cheese, thinly sliced

3 tablespoons coarsely chopped fresh basil

Salt and pepper to taste

1 tablespoon olive oil

1 tablespoon balsamic vinegar

1 In shallow bowl or plate, layer or arrange tomatoes, mozzarella, basil and season to taste. Drizzle with olive oil and balsamic vinegar. Serve immediately.

NUTRITIONAL INFO:

Calories 109

Calories from Fat 69%

Fat 9g

Saturated Fat 3g

Cholesterol 17mg

Sodium 18mg

Carbohydrates 4g

Dietary Fiber 1g

Total Sugars 3g

Protein 4g

Dietary Exchanges:
1 vegetable, 1/2 lean meat, 1 1/2 fat

CHICKEN PARMESAN CASSEROLE

Makes 8 servings

2 tablespoons olive oil

1 teaspoon minced garlic

2 pounds boneless skinless chicken breast cutlets pounded thin

2 cups marinara sauce

1 tablespoon dried basil leaves

1 1/4 cups shredded part-skim mozzarella cheese, divided

1/4 cup grated Parmesan cheese

1 (5-ounce) package garlic croutons

1 Preheat oven 350°F.

2 In 3-quart oblong baking dish, mix oil and garlic. Lay chicken breasts on top. Cover with marinara and sprinkle with basil.

3 Sprinkle with half mozzarella, all Parmesan, all croutons and remaining mozzarella. Bake 40 minutes or until chicken is done.

NUTRITIONAL INFO:

Calories 346

Calories from Fat 39%

Fat 15g

Saturated Fat 4g

Cholesterol 84mg

Sodium 724mg

Carbohydrates 19g

Dietary Fiber 1g

Total Sugars 3g

Protein 33g

Dietary Exchanges:
1 starch, 1 vegetable, 4 lean meat, 1/2 fat

CHOCOLATE ITALIAN CREAM CAKE

My absolute indulgent favorite!

See page 182

SOUTHWESTERN SOIRÉE

Southwestern Slaw

Chile Con Queso

Easy Beef Enchiladas

CHILE CON QUESO

Everyone's all-time favorite Mexican dip now can be made simply and sensationally in a moment's notice. Serve heated with chips.

Makes 12 (1/4-cup) servings

1 onion, chopped

1/2 teaspoon minced garlic

1/2 cup light beer

1 1/4 cups skim milk, divided

3 tablespoons cornstarch

1 1/2 cups shredded reduced-fat sharp Cheddar cheese

1 (10-ounce) can diced tomatoes and green chilies, drained

1/3 cup chopped green onions

1 teaspoon ground cumin

1 teaspoon chili powder

1 In large nonstick pot coated with nonstick cooking spray, sauté onion and garlic until onion is tender.

2 Add beer and cook until reduced slightly, about 1 minute. Add 1 cup milk and heat until almost boiling.

3 Meanwhile, in small bowl, whisk remaining 1/4 cup milk and cornstarch. Add to pot, and cook, stirring, until bubbling and thickened. Reduce heat and add remaining ingredients, stirring until cheese is melted.

NUTRITIONAL INFO:

Calories 64

Calories from Fat 31%

Fat 2g

Saturated Fat 2g

Cholesterol 8mg

Sodium 196mg

Carbohydrates 6g

Dietary Fiber 1g

Total Sugars 2g

Protein 5g

Dietary Exchanges:
1/2 starch,
1/2 lean meat

SOUTHWESTERN SLAW

A memorable Mexican cole slaw.
See page 120

EASY BEEF ENCHILADAS

 D

Ridiculously easy and absolutely delicious dinner pronto!

Makes 10 enchiladas

NUTRITIONAL INFO:
Calories 64
Calories from Fat 31%
Fat 2g
Saturated Fat 2g
Cholesterol 8mg
Sodium 196mg
Carbohydrates 6g
Dietary Fiber 1g
Total Sugars 2g
Protein 5g
Dietary Exchanges:
1/2 starch,
1/2 lean meat

1 pound ground sirloin

2 teaspoons chili powder

1 cup salsa

1 cup corn

1 cup packed fresh baby spinach

1 1/2 cups shredded reduced-fat Mexican-blend cheese

10 (6–8-inch) flour tortillas, room temperature

1 1/2 cups enchilada sauce (found in can)

1 bunch green onions, chopped

1 Preheat oven 350°F. Coat 13 x 9 x 2-inch baking dish with nonstick cooking spray.

2 In large nonstick skillet, cook meat 6–8 minutes or until meat is done. Drain any excess fat.

3 Add chili powder, salsa, corn, and spinach; continue cooking about 5 minutes. Remove from heat, set aside.

4 Spoon about 1/4 cup meat mixture and 1 tablespoon cheese onto a tortilla. Roll and place seam side down in prepared baking dish. Repeat with remaining tortillas.

5 Pour enchilada sauce evenly over filled tortillas in baking dish and sprinkle with any remaining cheese and green onions Bake, covered with foil, 20 minutes or until thoroughly heated.

CHINESE TAKE OUT

Tossed Asian Salad with Wasabi Vinaigrette (pg 84)
Beef & Broccoli Stir-Fry (pg 85)
Stir-Fry Rice (pg 86)

Tossed Asian Salad with
Wasabi Vinaigrette

Stir-Fry Rice

Beef & Broccoli Stir-Fry

TOSSED ASIAN SALAD *with* WASABI VINAIGRETTE

 D

Wasabi Vinaigrette adds punch to this fantastic crunchy combination of slaw and spinach topped with toasty almonds. Combine salad mixture, make vinaigrette, refrigerate and toss together to serve.

Makes 4 (1-cup) servings

2 cups baby spinach

2 cups coleslaw (found in bag)

1 (8-ounce) can water chestnuts, chopped or sliced, drained

1/2 cup diced red bell pepper

1 bunch green onions, chopped

Wasabi Vinaigrette, (recipe follows)

1/4 cup sliced almonds, toasted

1 In large bowl, combine spinach, coleslaw, water chestnuts, red pepper and green onions. Toss with Wasabi Vinaigrette (see recipe) to lightly coat. Divide on plates and sprinkle with almonds.

WASABI VINAIGRETTE

Makes 1/3 cup vinaigrette

1 tablespoon Dijon mustard

1/2 teaspoon wasabi

1/4 cup seasoned rice or white vinegar

1 teaspoon sesame oil

2 tablespoons canola oil

1 In small bowl, whisk together all ingredients until smooth and well combined.

NUTRITIONAL INFO:

Calories 180

Calories from Fat 57%

Fat 12g

Saturated Fat 1g

Cholesterol 0mg

Sodium 313mg

Carbohydrates 17g

Dietary Fiber 6g

Total Sugars 9g

Protein 3g

Dietary Exchanges:
3 vegetable, 2 1/2 fat

TERRIFIC TIP

Wasabi can be found in powder form in a small tin can in Asian section of grocery store or fresh where sushi is sold.

BEEF & BROCCOLI STIR-FRY

No need for Chinese take-out when you can whip up this quick and tasty stir-fry. Serve with rice.

Makes 4 servings

2 tablespoons low-sodium soy sauce

1 tablespoon honey

1 1/2 teaspoons ground ginger

1 teaspoon minced garlic

2 tablespoons cornstarch, divided

2 tablespoons plus 1 cup fat-free chicken broth, divided

1 pound flank steak, trimmed of fat and cut into strips
   (sirloin or round steak may be used)

1 onion, coarsely chopped

4 cups broccoli florets

1 green or red bell pepper, seeded and cut into strips

1/2 cup chopped green onions

1 (8-ounce) can sliced water chestnuts, drained

1. In glass dish or plastic bag, combine soy sauce, honey, ginger, garlic, 1 tablespoon cornstarch and 2 tablespoons chicken broth. Add sliced meat and marinate in refrigerator, covered, 1 hour, time permitting.

2. In large shallow skillet coated with nonstick cooking spray, stir-fry meat few minutes until browned. Add onion, broccoli, and pepper cooking over medium-high heat 5-7 minutes or until tender.

3. In small bowl mix together remaining 1 cup chicken broth and 1 tablespoon cornstarch. Add to skillet; bring to boil, stirring, until mixture slightly thickens and meat done.

4. Stir in green onions and water chestnuts.

NUTRITIONAL INFO:
Calories 272
Calories from Fat 23%
Fat 7g
Saturated Fat 3g
Cholesterol 48mg
Sodium 540mg
Carbohydrates 25g
Dietary Fiber 6g
Total Sugars 11g
Protein 28g
Dietary Exchanges:
3 vegetable, 1/2 other carbohydrate,
3 lean meat

TERRIFIC TIP

The best cuts of beef for stir-frying are flank steak and sirloin, which are more tender and full-flavored.

To make slicing beef into strips easier, freeze uncooked meat 15-30 minutes. To easily cut meat, use kitchen scissors.

STIR-FRY RICE

 D

Freeze leftover rice to prepare this fast cooking terrific side and add to any meal or serve as vegetarian entrée.

Makes 6 (1-cup) servings

2 tablespoons canola oil

1/2 cup chopped onion

1/2 pound sliced mushrooms

1 teaspoon minced garlic

2 egg whites, beaten

3 cups cooked rice (white or brown)

2 tablespoons low-sodium soy sauce

3 tablespoons seasoned rice vinegar

1/3 cup fat-free vegetable or chicken broth

2 teaspoons finely chopped fresh ginger or
   1 teaspoon ground ginger

1/2 cup shelled edamame, (if frozen, thaw)

1/2 cup chopped green onions

1 tablespoon sesame seeds, toasted, optional

NUTRITIONAL INFO:
Calories 196
Calories from Fat 26%
Fat 6g
Saturated Fat 0g
Cholesterol 0mg
Sodium 303mg
Carbohydrates 30g
Dietary Fiber 2g
Total Sugars 5g
Protein 7g
Dietary Exchanges:
2 starch, 1 fat

TERRIFIC TIP

Be creative and add whatever veggies you have or even leftover, seafood, chicken or meat.

You can find toasted sesame seeds in the spice section.

1 In large nonstick skillet, heat oil and sauté onion, mushrooms, and garlic 5-7 minutes. Add egg whites and rice, stirring and cooking until egg whites are done.

2 Add soy sauce, vinegar, broth, and ginger cooking and stirring until heated, about 3 minutes. Add edamame and green onions, stirring until well heated. Sprinkle with sesame seeds, if desired.

LOUISIANA LAGNIAPPE

Red Beans & Rice

Yummy Yam Quick Bread

Crab Cakes

Cream Cheese Bread Pudding

Butter Pecan Roasted Sweet Potatoes

Crabmeat Brie Dip

YUMMY YAM QUICK BREAD

  D

Yes, you read the recipe correctly, as these few ingredients create one of my very favorite moist lip-smacking breads.

Makes 16 servings

1 (18.25-ounce) box spice cake mix

1 teaspoon ground cinnamon

1 (15-ounce) can sweet potatoes, drained and mashed

1/2 cup water

Crumble Topping, (recipe follows) optional

1 Preheat oven 350° F. Coat 9x5x3-inch loaf pan with nonstick cooking spray.

2 In mixing bowl, mix together spice cake mix, cinnamon, sweet potatoes and water just until combined. Transfer to prepared pan. Sprinkle with Crumble Topping (see recipe), if desired.

3 Bake 40-50 minutes or until toothpick inserted in the middle comes out clean.

CRUMBLE TOPPING

1/4 cup light brown sugar

1/4 cup all-purpose flour

1/3 cup chopped pecans

2 tablespoons butter, melted

1 teaspoon vanilla extract

1 In small bowl, mix together all ingredients until crumbly.

NUTRITIONAL INFO:
Without optional Crumble Topping
Calories 157
Calories from Fat 15%
Fat 3g
Saturated Fat 1g
Cholesterol 0mg
Sodium 221mg
Carbohydrates 30g
Dietary Fiber 1g
Total Sugars 15g
Protein 2g
Dietary Exchanges:
2 other carbohydrate, 1/2 fat

NUTRITIONAL INFO:
With optional Crumble Topping
Calories 207
Calories from Fat 25%
Fat 6g
Saturated Fat 2g
Cholesterol 4mg
Sodium 235mg
Carbohydrates 38g
Dietary Fiber 1g
Total Sugars 19g
Protein 2g
Dietary Exchanges:
2 1/2 other carbohydrate, 1 fat

1 (15-ounce) can sweet potatoes = 1 cup mashed cooked Louisiana yams (sweet potatoes) so if you have leftover baked sweet potatoes, here's your sweet solution

TERRIFIC TIP

BUTTER PECAN ROASTED SWEET POTATOES

Candied yams at their finest with a surprise kick.

See page 32

CRABMEAT BRIE DIP

Divine, creamy, and rich tasting, taking minutes to make.
Crabmeat and Brie — Need I say more?

See page 58

RED BEANS & RICE

A nutritional bargain and delightfully delicious high protein and fiber meal plus it's easy!

Makes 10 (1/2-cup) servings

8 ounces reduced-fat sausage, sliced into
    1/2-inch thick rounds

1 onion, chopped

1/3 cup chopped celery

1 teaspoon minced garlic

3 (16-ounce) cans red kidney beans, rinsed and drained

1/2 cup tomato sauce

1 1/2 cups fat-free chicken or vegetable broth

1/3 cup chopped parsley

1/2 cup chopped green onions

NUTRITIONAL INFO:
Calories 145
Calories from Fat 4%
Fat 1g
Saturated Fat 0g
Cholesterol 5mg
Sodium 534mg
Carbohydrates 28g
Dietary Fiber 9g
Total Sugars 5g
Protein 10g
Dietary Exchanges:
2 starch, 1 lean meat

1. In large nonstick skillet coated with nonstick cooking spray, cook sausage over medium heat, stirring, until crispy brown. Set aside.

2. In large nonstick pot coated with nonstick cooking spray, sauté onion, celery, and garlic until tender, 5–7 minutes.

3. Add beans, tomato sauce, broth, and sausage. Bring to boil, reduce heat, and cover. Simmer 8–10 minutes, or until thickened, mashing some of the beans with fork.

4. Add parsley and green onions, and continue cooking several more minutes.

CRAB CAKES

 D

As a huge crab cake fan, this easy-to prepare recipe promises to tantalize your taste buds. The secret to good crab cakes is quality crabmeat and minimum filler.

Makes 8 crab cakes

1 cup panko bread crumbs, divided

1 egg

2 tablespoons skim milk

1/2 cup chopped green onions

2 teaspoons Dijon mustard

1 teaspoon Worcestershire sauce

1/4 teaspoon hot sauce

1 (16-ounce) container lump or white crabmeat, picked through for shells

1 tablespoon olive oil

NUTRITIONAL INFO:

Calories 117

Calories from Fat 25%

Fat 3g

Saturated Fat 1g

Cholesterol 66mg

Sodium 272mg

Carbohydrates 7g

Dietary Fiber 1g

Total Sugars 1g

Protein 14g

Dietary Exchanges:
1/2 starch, 2 lean meat

1   In bowl, mix 1/2 cup panko crumbs, egg, milk, green onions, mustard, Worcestershire, and hot sauce mixing well with fork. Carefully, fold in crabmeat and with hands mold into eight crab cakes.

2   Coat crab cakes with remaining 1/2 cup panko, pressing gently to make crumbs adhere. Refrigerate 30 minutes or time permitting.

3   In large nonstick skillet, heat oil and cook crab cakes 3-4 minutes, spray nonstick cooking spray on top crab cake, flip and cook another 3-4 minutes or until done.

TERRIFIC TIP

Serve as a main course, or make miniatures for appetizers.

HORSERADISH SAUCE

Cool sauce with a bite of flavor.

6 (2-tablespoon) servings

1 tablespoon light mayonnaise

1/3 cup nonfat plain yogurt

1 tablespoon prepared horseradish

1 tablespoon lemon juice

2 tablespoons finely chopped onion

1   In small bowl, combine all ingredients.

NUTRITIONAL INFO:

Calories 64

Calories from Fat 31%

Fat 2g

Saturated Fat 2g

Cholesterol 8mg

Sodium 196mg

Carbohydrates 6g

Dietary Fiber 1g

Total Sugars 2g

Protein 5g

Dietary Exchanges:
1/2 starch,
1/2 lean meat

CREAM CHEESE BREAD PUDDING

Bread pudding, always a popular dessert, with this cream cheese topping reaches new heights!

Makes 16 servings

1 (16-ounce) loaf French bread

2 eggs, divided

4 egg whites, divided

1 cup sugar, divided

1 teaspoon vanilla extract

1 teaspoon imitation butter flavoring

3 cups skim milk

1 teaspoon ground cinnamon

1 (8-ounce) package reduced-fat cream cheese

1 Preheat oven 350°F. Coat 13x9x2-inch baking dish with nonstick cooking spray.

2 Cut French bread into 1-inch squares. Place bread in prepared dish.

3 In large bowl, lightly beat together 1 egg and 3 egg whites. Add 1/2 cup sugar, vanilla, butter flavoring; mix well. Slowly add milk to egg mixture, mixing well. Pour over bread squares. Sprinkle mixture with cinnamon.

4 In mixing bowl, beat cream cheese with remaining 1/2 cup sugar. Add remaining egg and egg white, blending until smooth. Spread mixture evenly over soaked bread.

5 Bake, uncovered, 45 minutes or until firm. Let cool slightly before serving.

NUTRITIONAL INFO:

Calories 197

Calories from Fat 19%

Fat 4g

Saturated Fat 2g

Cholesterol 34mg

Sodium 248mg

Carbohydrates 31g

Dietary Fiber 1g

Total Sugars 16g

Protein 8g

Dietary Exchanges:
1 starch, 1 other carbohydrate, 1/2 lean meat

TERRIFIC TIP

Serving Option: Serve with fresh fruit.

HOLIDAY HEROS

Cranberry Avocado Mixed Green Salad (pg 93)
Cranberry Nut Oatmeal Bread (pg 94)
Sweet Potato Casserole with Praline Topping (pg 95)

Spinach & Artichoke Casserole (pg 96)
Red Velvet Cheesecake (pg 178)
Blonde Brownies (pg 97)

Blonde Brownies

Cranberry Avocado Mixed Green Salad

Sweet Potato Casserole with Praline Topping

Spinach & Artichoke Casserole

Red Velvet Cheesecake

Cranberry Nut Oatmeal Bread

CRANBERRY AVOCADO MIXED GREEN SALAD

Tart cranberries, buttery avocados and nutty pecans combine to make one delicious, anytime salad.

Makes 6-8 servings

1 (9-ounce) bag baby spinach

1 (9-ounce) bag mixed greens

2 medium avocados, chopped

1/3 cup dried cranberries

1/3 cup pecans, toasted

1 tablespoon sugar

1 tablespoon poppy seeds

1 tablespoon sesame seeds

1/2 teaspoon paprika

2 teaspoons ground mustard

2 tablespoons minced red onion

1/2 cup seasoned rice or white vinegar

1/3 cup olive oil

1 In large bowl, mix together spinach, mixed greens, avocados, cranberries, and pecans.

2 In another small bowl, whisk together remaining ingredients for vinaigrette. Toss together when ready to serve.

NUTRITIONAL INFO:

Calories 262

Calories from Fat 69%

Fat 22g

Saturated Fat 3g

Cholesterol 0mg

Sodium 228mg

Carbohydrates 18g

Dietary Fiber 6g

Total Sugars 11g

Protein 4g

Dietary Exchanges:
1 vegetable,
1 other carbohydrate,
4 fat

TERRIFIC TIP

Not only are avocados buttery and delicious they are also packed with nutrients.

Don't have ground mustard, use Dijon or yellow mustard.

CRANBERRY NUT OATMEAL BREAD

This festive sweet and tart oatmeal grainy bread uses the whole bag of cranberries, as I always hated a small amount of cranberries left in a bag.

Makes 16 slices

2 1/2 cups all-purpose flour

1 teaspoon baking powder

1 teaspoon baking soda

1/2 teaspoon ground cinnamon

1 cup old-fashioned oatmeal

1/2 cup honey

1/2 cup light brown sugar

1/3 cup canola oil

2 eggs

1/2 cup skim milk

1 teaspoon vanilla extract

1 (12-ounce) package fresh cranberries, chopped

2/3 cup chopped pecans

1. Preheat oven 350°F. Coat 9x5x 3-inch loaf pan with nonstick cooking spray.

2. In bowl, stir together flour, baking powder, baking soda, cinnamon and oatmeal.

3. In large bowl, mix together honey, brown sugar, oil, eggs, milk and vanilla. Stir in flour mixture until moistened. Stir in cranberries and pecans.

4. Pour batter into prepared pan. Bake 40-45 minutes, or until toothpick inserted in center comes out clean.

NUTRITIONAL INFO:
Calories 244

Calories from Fat 33%

Fat 9g

Saturated Fat 1g

Cholesterol 23mg

Sodium 119mg

Carbohydrates 37g

Dietary Fiber 2g

Total Sugars 17g

Protein 5g

Dietary Exchanges:
1 1/2 starch, 1 other carbohydrate, 1 1/2 fat

TERRIFIC TIP

Cranberries freeze up to one year so stock up on fresh cranberries while they are plentiful during the holiday season.

SWEET POTATO CASSEROLE
with PRALINE TOPPING

Volunteer to bring this simple and fabulous sweet potato dish for your next holiday meal. Don't save for only the holidays — eat all year round!

Makes 12 (1/2-cup) servings

3 cups cooked mashed peeled Louisiana yams (sweet potatoes), about 3-4 sweet potatoes

2/3 cup of 1 (14-ounce) can fat-free sweetened condensed milk

2 egg whites

1/4 cup orange juice

Praline Topping (recipe follows)

1 Preheat oven 350°F. Coat 2-quart casserole with nonstick cooking spray.

2 In bowl, cream together all ingredients except the topping with potato masher or mixer until blended. Transfer to prepared dish and sprinkle with Praline Topping (see recipe).

3 Bake 40-45 minutes or until thoroughly heated and topping is brown and crumbly.

PRALINE TOPPING

2/3 cup light brown sugar

1/3 cup all-purpose flour

1/2 teaspoon ground cinnamon

1/4 cup butter, melted

1 teaspoon vanilla extract

1 cup chopped pecans

1 In bowl, mix together brown sugar, flour, and cinnamon. Stir in butter, vanilla, and pecans until crumbly.

NUTRITIONAL INFO:

Calories 274

Calories from Fat 34%

Fat 11g

Saturated Fat 3g

Cholesterol 12mg

Sodium 87mg

Carbohydrates 42g

Dietary Fiber 3g

Total Sugars 28g

Protein 4g

Dietary Exchanges:
1 starch, 2 other carbohydrate, 2 fat

TERRIFIC TIP

Canned (drained) or fresh sweet potatoes may be used for this recipe. See page in Basics (pg 123) for directions to baking a sweet potato.

SPINACH & ARTICHOKE CASSEROLE

Simply spinach and artichokes in a quick creamy casserole — doesn't get much better than this!

Makes 4 (1-cup) servings

2 (10-ounce) packages frozen chopped spinach

1/2 pound sliced mushrooms

2 tablespoons light mayonnaise

3/4 cup nonfat sour cream

1 (14-ounce) can quartered artichoke hearts, drained

1/3 cup grated Parmesan cheese

Salt and pepper to taste

NUTRITIONAL INFO:

Calories 172

Calories from Fat 24%

Fat 5g

Saturated Fat 2g

Cholesterol 16mg

Sodium 471mg

Carbohydrates 21g

Dietary Fiber 5g

Total Sugars 6g

Protein 14g

Dietary Exchanges:
1/2 starch, 2 vegetable,
1 lean meat

1 Preheat oven 350°F. Coat baking dish with nonstick cooking spray.

2 Cook spinach according to package directions; drain well.

3 In small nonstick skillet coated with nonstick cooking spray, sauté mushrooms until tender.

4 In large bowl, combine spinach, mushrooms, mayonnaise, sour cream, artichokes, Parmesan cheese and season to taste. If desired, sprinkle top with Parmesan cheese. Bake 30 minutes or until bubbly.

TERRIFIC TIP

Try sautéing the mushrooms in white wine or sherry to kick up the flavor in this dish. This recipe may also be served as Spinach Artichoke Dip with chips.

RED VELVET CHEESECAKE

I love any dessert that has "Red Velvet" in it, and especially cheesecake!
See page 178

BLONDE BROWNIES

This is my go-to holiday bar cookie for Halloween, Thanksgiving, Christmas, Valentine's Day or Easter to use holiday themed chocolate coated candies.

Makes 48 squares

1/2 cup butter, melted

1 2/3 cups light brown sugar

2 eggs

1 tablespoon vanilla extract

2 cups all-purpose flour

2 teaspoons baking powder

1/4 teaspoon baking soda

1/4 cup skim milk

1 cup holiday colored chocolate coated candies

1. Preheat oven 350°F. Coat 13x9x2-inch baking pan with nonstick cooking spray.

2. In large bowl, combine butter and brown sugar. Add eggs, one at a time, beating well. Add vanilla.

3. In bowl, combine flour, baking powder and baking soda. Gradually stir into sugar mixture alternately with milk. Stir in chocolate candies. Transfer to pan.

4. Bake 18-20 minutes or until toothpick inserted in center comes out clean. Don't overcook.

NUTRITIONAL INFO:

Calories 91

Calories from Fat 30%

Fat 3g

Saturated Fat 2g

Cholesterol 13mg

Sodium 49mg

Carbohydrates 15g

Dietary Fiber 0g

Total Sugars 10g

Protein 1g

Dietary Exchanges:
1 other carbohydrate, 1/2 fat

TERRIFIC TIP

You don't need a mixer for this recipe as you can stir everything easily in a bowl.

You can use semisweet or butterscotch chips year round.

Chicken Pot Pie (pg 105)

4

RAPID ROTISSERIE CHICKEN RECIPES

MEXICAN CHICKEN ORZO SALAD

D

NUTRITIONAL INFO:

Calories 258

Calories from Fat 14%

Fat 4g

Saturated Fat 1g

Cholesterol 32mg

Sodium 170mg

Carbohydrates 39g

Dietary Fiber 2g

Total Sugars 4g

Protein 17g

Dietary Exchanges:
2 1/2 starch,
1 1/2 lean meat

TERRIFIC TIP

Orzo pasta, a larger rice shaped grain, can be found in the pasta section of your grocery and is a great option for pasta salads. Any small pasta may be substituted.

A great group-pleasing pasta salad with tomatoes, corn and chicken tossed with a light southwestern lime vinaigrette.

Makes 8 (1-cup) servings

4 cups cooked orzo pasta

2 cups chopped skinless rotisserie chicken breast

1 cup chopped tomatoes

1 cup frozen corn, thawed

1/4 cup chopped red onion

1/2 cup chopped green onions

1 tablespoon Dijon mustard

2 tablespoons lime juice

1 tablespoon olive oil

1 tablespoon chopped jalapeño pepper

1/2 teaspoon chili powder

1/2 teaspoon ground cumin

1 In large bowl, combine orzo, chicken, tomatoes, corn, red onion and green onions.

2 In small bowl, whisk Dijon, lime juice, olive oil, jalapeno, chili powder and cumin. Pour dressing over pasta mixture, tossing to mix.

HARVEST CHICKEN SALAD

Perfect blend of seasoned chicken, sweet tart cranberries, toasty walnuts, and feta combined with a light creamy dressing.

Makes 5 (1-cup) servings

2 cups chopped skinless rotisserie chicken breast

1/3 cup diced red onion

2 tablespoons dried cranberries

1/4 cup chopped pecans or walnuts, toasted

1/4 cup crumbled reduced-fat feta cheese

2 cups small apple chunks (green apples)

1 tablespoon lemon juice

1/3 cup nonfat plain Greek yogurt

1 tablespoon light mayonnaise

Dash sugar

1 In bowl, combine chicken, onion, cranberries, walnuts, and feta. Toss apple with lemon juice and add to chicken mixture.

2 In small bowl, mix together yogurt, mayonnaise, and sugar. Carefully mix with chicken mixture.

D

NUTRITIONAL INFO:

Calories 192

Calories from Fat 34%

Fat 7g

Saturated Fat 2g

Cholesterol 53mg

Sodium 320mg

Carbohydrates 12g

Dietary Fiber 2g

Total Sugars 9g

Protein 20g

Dietary Exchanges:
1 fruit, 3 lean meat

TERRIFIC TIP

You can use red, green or a combination of apples.

CHICKEN FAJITA PIZZA

 D

Fajita and pizza together in one recipe can only mean instantaneous deliciousness.

Makes 8 servings

NUTRITIONAL INFO:

Calories 219

Calories from Fat 26%

Fat 6g

Saturated Fat 2g

Cholesterol 41mg

Sodium 546mg

Carbohydrates 21g

Dietary Fiber 1g

Total Sugars 4g

Protein 19g

Dietary Exchanges:
1 1/2 starch,
2 lean meat

2 cups shredded skinless, rotisserie chicken breast

1 teaspoon chili powder

1 medium onion, thinly sliced

1 medium green bell pepper, seeded and thinly sliced into strips

1 (10-13.8-ounce) can refrigerated pizza crust

2/3 cup picante sauce

1 1/4 cups shredded reduced-fat Mexican blend cheese

1 Preheat oven 425° F. degrees. Coat pizza pan with nonstick cooking spray.

2 In bowl, combine chicken with chili powder; set aside. In large skillet coated with nonstick cooking spray, sauté onion and green pepper, cooking until crisp tender.

3 Unroll dough and place in pan; starting at center, press out with hands. Bake 6 minutes or until light golden brown. Remove from oven and spoon chicken and onion mixture over partially baked crust. Spoon picante sauce over chicken and sprinkle with cheese. Return to oven and bake 10-12 minutes.

TERRIFIC TIP

Can use a Boboli crust or can pick up your favorite prepared pizza crust.

CHICKEN TORTILLA SOUP

Looking for a last minute meal? This one-pot soup rocks!

Makes 8 (1-cup) servings

1 onion, chopped

1 teaspoon minced garlic

1 red bell pepper, seeded and chopped

1 teaspoon ground cumin

1 teaspoon dried oregano leaves

2 cups shredded skinless rotisserie chicken breast

5 cups fat-free chicken broth

1 cup frozen corn

1 (4-ounce) can green chilies

1 cup red enchilada sauce

1/2 cup chopped green onions

1. In large pot coated with nonstick cooking spray, sauté onion, garlic and bell pepper until tender.

2. Add cumin, oregano, chicken, broth, corn, green chilies and enchilada sauce. Bring to boil, reduce, and simmer 15 minutes. To serve, sprinkle with green onions.

NUTRITIONAL INFO:

Calories 106

Calories from Fat 18%

Fat 2g

Saturated Fat 0g

Cholesterol 32mg

Sodium 928mg

Carbohydrates 10g

Dietary Fiber 2g

Total Sugars 3g

Protein 12g

Dietary Exchanges:
1/2 starch, 1 vegetable,
1 1/2 lean meat

TERRIFIC TIP

For a punch of nutrition, toss chopped zucchini and white or black beans into soup.

Serve with chopped avocado and cheese.

CHICKEN & DUMPLINGS

With rotisserie chicken, canned broth and drop dumplings, this favorite comfort food becomes an effortless one-dish meal.

Makes 8 (1-cup) servings

NUTRITIONAL INFO:

Calories 218

Calories from Fat 23%

Fat 6g

Saturated Fat 1g

Cholesterol 32mg

Sodium 1207mg

Carbohydrates 28g

Dietary Fiber 2g

Total Sugars 4g

Protein 15g

Dietary Exchanges:
1 1/2 starch, 1 vegetable, 1 1/2 lean meat

TERRIFIC TIP

A short-cut for dumplings: cut flaky biscuits into fourths and drop into boiling broth or you can even use flour tortillas cut into fourths.

You can slice carrots — but I find baby carrots a time-saver.

---

1 onion, chopped

1 1/2 cups baby carrots

1/2 teaspoon minced garlic

1/4 cup all-purpose flour

6 cups fat-free chicken broth, divided

1/2 teaspoon dried thyme leaves

2 cups chopped skinless rotisserie chicken breast

2 cups biscuit baking mix

2/3 cup skim milk

Salt and pepper to taste

1. In large nonstick pot coated with nonstick cooking spray, sauté onion, carrots, and garlic over medium heat until tender.

2. In small cup, stir flour and 1/3 cup chicken broth, mixing until smooth. Gradually add flour mixture and remaining broth to pot; bring to boil. Add thyme and chicken.

3. In bowl, stir together biscuit baking mix and milk. Drop the mixture by spoonfuls into boiling broth.

4. Return to boil, reduce heat, and cook, covered, carefully stirring occasionally, 15-20 minutes or until dumplings are done. Season to taste. If soup is too thick, add more chicken broth.

CHICKEN POT PIES

Nothing beats southern comfort food like a good chicken pot pie. Make individual servings or in one dish.

Makes 6 (3-small pot pie) servings

1 cup chopped onion

1 cup chopped celery

1 cup sliced baby carrots

2 tablespoons cornstarch

1 1/2 cups fat-free chicken broth, divided

1/2 cup evaporated skimmed milk

1/2 teaspoon dried thyme leaves

2 cups chopped skinless rotisserie chicken breast

18 refrigerated canned biscuits

1. Preheat oven 400°F. Coat muffin pans with nonstick cooking spray.

2. In nonstick skillet coated with nonstick cooking spray, sauté onion, celery, and carrots until tender, stirring.

3. In small cup, add cornstarch to 1/2 cup chicken broth, mixing well. Pour into skillet, stirring. Gradually add remaining chicken broth, stirring and cooking over medium heat until thickened and bubbly. Add evaporated milk and thyme. Return to boil, add chicken, cooking until mixture is thickened and bubbly.

4. While filling is cooking, pat biscuits into large circles with palm of your hand and set in muffin pans. Once filling is done, spoon about 1/4 cup filling into each biscuit and pull sides of biscuit over the top. Repeat until all biscuits are filled. Bake 10-12 minutes or until biscuits are golden brown.

NUTRITIONAL INFO:

Calories 282

Calories from Fat 20%

Fat 6g

Saturated Fat 1g

Cholesterol 43mg

Sodium 961mg

Carbohydrates 37g

Dietary Fiber 2g

Total Sugars 8g

Protein 20g

Dietary Exchanges:
2 starch, 1 vegetable, 2 lean meat

TERRIFIC TIP

Try adding mixed vegetables or sweet potatoes to the filling. To lower sodium, use low-sodium chicken broth for diabetic-friendly recipe.

In a hurry, spread filling into baking dish and top with biscuits (one can biscuits will do) as in photo.

QUICK CHICKEN RICE CASSEROLE

These five ingredients make a memorable family-pleasing dish that we devoured in no time at all.

Makes 8 (1-cup) servings

2 cups chopped skinless rotisserie chicken breasts

2 (4-ounce) cans diced green chilies

2 cups fat-free sour cream

Salt and pepper to taste

3 cups cooked rice (or brown), divided

2 cups shredded reduced-fat Mexican blend cheese, divided

1 Preheat oven 350°F. Coat 2-quart baking dish with nonstick cooking spray.

2 In large bowl, combine chicken, green chilies, sour cream, and season to taste.

3 Spread half of rice in prepared dish. Cover with half sour cream mixture, sprinkle with half the cheese. Repeat layers. Bake 30-40 minutes or until well heated.

NUTRITIONAL INFO:

Calories 274

Calories from Fat 23%

Fat 7g

Saturated Fat 4g

Cholesterol 59mg

Sodium 495mg

Carbohydrates 29g

Dietary Fiber 1g

Total Sugars 4g

Protein 23g

Dietary Exchanges:
2 starch, 3 lean meat

TERRIFIC TIP

For a step-saver: freeze leftover rice to use for this quick dinner.

MEXICAN CHICKEN RICE DISH

An exceptional combination of layers and flavors makes a fiesta in your mouth. A hearty crowd pleaser.

Makes 8 (1 1/2-cup) servings

2 cups brown rice

3 cups chopped skinless rotisserie chicken breast

1 (15-ounce) can mild green enchilada sauce

1 (4-ounce) can sliced black olives, drained

1 (14 1/2-ounce) can diced tomatoes, drained

1 bunch green onions, chopped

1/2 cup nonfat plain yogurt

1 teaspoon ground cumin

1 (15-ounce) can black beans, drained and rinsed

2 cups reduced-fat shredded Cheddar cheese

1. Preheat oven 350°F. Coat 13x9x2-inch baking dish with nonstick cooking spray.

2. Cook rice according to package directions. Transfer to baking dish.

3. In large bowl, combine chicken, enchilada sauce, olives, tomatoes, green onions, yogurt, and cumin, mixing gently.

4. Layer black beans evenly on top of rice. Carefully spread chicken mixture over beans and sprinkle with cheese. Bake 20-30 minutes or until well heated and cheese is melted.

NUTRITIONAL INFO:

Calories 292

Calories from Fat 23%

Fat 7g

Saturated Fat 3g

Cholesterol 42mg

Sodium 679mg

Carbohydrates 34g

Dietary Fiber 5g

Total Sugars 3g

Protein 21g

Dietary Exchanges:
2 starch, 1 vegetable, 2 lean meat

TERRIFIC TIP

You can use brown or white rice.

STUFFED CHICKEN CAESAR SANDWICH

D

Everyone's favorite salad tossed with rotisserie chicken stuffed into crusty French bread makes a quick-chick sandwich.

Makes 6 sandwiches with (2/3-cup) chicken mixture

NUTRITIONAL INFO:

Calories 274

Calories from Fat 13%

Fat 4g

Saturated Fat 1g

Cholesterol 45mg

Sodium 550mg

Carbohydrates 37g

Dietary Fiber 3g

Total Sugars 4g

Protein 24g

Dietary Exchanges:
2 1/2 starch,
2 1/2 lean meat

1 (16-ounce) loaf French bread or 6 small loaves
   (whole wheat may also be used)

1 large head romaine lettuce, torn into pieces (about 8 cups)

1/4 cup grated Parmesan cheese

2 cups chopped skinless rotisserie chicken breast

1/2 cup plain nonfat yogurt

1/2 teaspoon minced garlic

2 tablespoons lemon juice

1 teaspoon vinegar

1 teaspoon Worcestershire sauce

1 teaspoon Dijon mustard

TERRIFIC TIP

The Caesar dressing may be used on a salad.

1 If using large French bread, cut into 6 sections. Hollow out inside and discard extra bread. Toast hollowed out bread until light brown.

2 In bowl, combine lettuce, cheese, and chicken.

3 In small bowl, whisk together remaining ingredients. Toss with chicken mixture; stuff into each hollow toasted bread section. Serve.

CHICKEN STIR-FRY LETTUCE WRAPS

Fast and fantastic, this enjoyable light meal with Asian flavors comes together easily with cooked chicken, bell pepper, edamame and sweet mango with a super sauce.

Makes 8 (1/2-cup filling) wraps

1 onion, halved and thinly sliced

1 red bell pepper, seeded and thinly sliced

1 teaspoon minced garlic

1 1/2 teaspoons grated fresh ginger

Hearty dash red pepper flakes

1/2 cup shelled edamame

1 tablespoon low-sodium soy sauce

3 tablespoons seasoned rice vinegar

1 teaspoon cornstarch, mixed with 1 tablespoon water

2 cups chopped skinless rotisserie chicken breast

1 cup chopped mango

2 tablespoons chopped peanuts

Boston or red tip lettuce leaves

1 In large nonstick skillet, sauté onion and bell pepper, cooking until onion is almost tender, about 5 minutes. Add garlic, ginger, red pepper flakes and edamame; stirring, about 1 minute.

2 Stir in soy sauce, vinegar, and cornstarch mixture, heating mixture until thickens. Remove from heat and add chicken, mango and peanuts. Spoon mixture onto lettuce and wrap.

D

NUTRITIONAL INFO:

Calories 104

Calories from Fat 24%

Fat 3g

Saturated Fat 0g

Cholesterol 32mg

Sodium 172mg

Carbohydrates 8g

Dietary Fiber 2g

Total Sugars 5g

Protein 13g

Dietary Exchanges:
1/2 other carbohydrate,
1 1/2 lean meat

TERRIFIC TIP

I serve my wraps with hoison sauce.

1/2 teaspoon ground ginger may be used for fresh ginger.

CHICKEN CHIPOTLE
TACOS *with* AVOCADO SALSA

D

TERRIFIC TIP

Chipotle peppers found in Mexican section of the grocery, have a spicy smoky flavor — don't have them or don't like them — leave the pepper out and add 1 teaspoon chili powder — tacos will be great either way.

*Photo on cookbook cover.

Shredded chicken in a smoky fiery sauce, topped with refreshing cool avocado salsa makes an outstanding combo.

Makes 8 tacos with heaping 1/3 cup filling, 3 tablespoons salsa

1/4 cup chopped red onion

1 teaspoon minced garlic

2-3 tablespoons chopped chipotle peppers (in can)

1 tablespoon honey

2 cups chopped tomatoes

1/4 cup chopped green onions

2 cups shredded skinless rotisserie chicken breast

Salt and pepper to taste

8 small flour tortillas, heated

Avocado Salsa, (recipe follows)

1. In large nonstick skillet, coated with nonstick cooking spray, sauté onion and garlic 3-5 minutes, stirring.

2. Add chipotle peppers, honey and tomatoes, cooking and stirring 5-7 minutes, or until slightly thickened.

3. Add green onions and chicken. Season to taste. Top each tortilla with chicken mixture and Avocado Salsa (see recipe).

AVOCADO SALSA

1/3 cup finely chopped cucumber

1/3 cup finely chopped red onion

1 large avocado, diced

1/2 teaspoon olive oil

1 tablespoon lime juice

Salt and pepper to taste

1. In bowl, combine all ingredients. Refrigerate until using.

Chicken Chipotle Tacos with Avocado Salsa (pg 110)

PULLED CHICKEN

Forget barbecue when you can instantly whip up this awesome and simple pulled chicken recipe.

Makes 4 (3/4-cup) servings

1 cup chopped onion

1/2 teaspoon minced garlic

2 tablespoons cider vinegar

1/2 cup chili sauce

1 tablespoon light brown sugar

1 teaspoon cocoa

1/2 teaspoon ground cumin

1/2 cup fat-free chicken broth

2 cups shredded skinless rotisserie chicken breast

1 In nonstick pot coated with nonstick cooking spray, sauté onion until tender. Add remaining ingredients except chicken, stirring. Cook about 7 minutes.

2 Add chicken and continue cooking until well heated.

NUTRITIONAL INFO:

Calories 170

Calories from Fat 14%

Fat 3g

Saturated Fat 1g

Cholesterol 63mg

Sodium 821mg

Carbohydrates 16g

Dietary Fiber 1g

Total Sugars 11g

Protein 21g

Dietary Exchanges:
1 other carbohydrate,
3 lean meat

TERRIFIC TIP

Chili sauce is found where ketchup is in the grocery. If you want to substitute ketchup for chili sauce, add 1 teaspoon chili powder to ketchup.

Serving option: Serve on sandwiches, sliders or as an entrée.

CHICKEN LASAGNA

Scrumptious chicken lasagna becomes simple in preparation with no-boil noodles and rotisserie chicken. Have fun adding other ingredients and using different flavored marinara sauces.

Makes 8-10 servings

2 (25-ounce) jars marinara sauce

1 (8-ounce) package no-boil lasagna noodles, divided

1 (15-ounce) container low-fat ricotta cheese

2 1/4 cups shredded part-skim mozzarella cheese, divided

1 rotisserie chicken, skin removed, cut into pieces (about 3 cups)

1 Preheat oven 375°F. Coat 13x9x2-inch pan with nonstick cooking spray.

2 Spread about 1 cup marinara sauce on bottom of pan. Top with one-third noodles, all the ricotta cheese, 1 cup mozzarella, half the chicken and 1 cup sauce. Repeat layering with one-third noodles, remaining chicken, and 1 cup mozzarella. Top with remaining noodles and sauce.

3 Bake, covered with foil, 1 hour. Uncover and top with remaining 1/4 cup cheese and continue cooking 5 minutes or until cheese is melted.

NUTRITIONAL INFO:

Calories 351

Calories from Fat 27%

Fat 10g

Saturated Fat 4g

Cholesterol 70mg

Sodium 907mg

Carbohydrates 36g

Dietary Fiber 4g

Total Sugars 13g

Protein 27g

Dietary Exchanges:
2 starch, 1 vegetable, 3 lean meat

TERRIFIC TIP

Try adding sliced mushrooms, baby spinach, and black olives to this basic recipe for added flair.

Asian Burgers (pg 116)

5

BUILDING ON BASICS

Burgers
Asian Burgers (pg 116)

Chicken Burgers (pg 116)

Snappy Salmon Burgers (pg 117)

Tacos
BBQ Shrimp Tacos (pg 118)

Pork Tacos with Pineapple Slaw (pg 119)

Fish Tacos with Southwestern Cole Slaw (pg 120)

Potatoes
Double Stuffed Potatoes (pg 121)

Southwestern Stuffed Potatoes (pg 122)

Sweet Potato Skins (pg 123)

Smashed Potato Mounds (pg 124)

Pizzas
BBQ Chicken Pizza (pg 125)

Mexican Meaty Pizza (pg 125)

Garden Pizza (pg 127)

ASIAN BURGERS

Like Asian food — wait until you try this burger!

Makes 4 Asian burgers

1 pound ground sirloin

1/4 cup panko bread crumbs

1/3 cup chopped green onions

1 egg, lightly beaten

1 teaspoon minced garlic

1 tablespoon hoisin sauce

1 tablespoon low-sodium soy sauce

1 tablespoon finely chopped fresh ginger or 1 teaspoon ground ginger

Pepper to taste

1 In large bowl, combine all ingredients until well mixed. Form into four patties. Grill or cook in skillet until done.

NUTRITIONAL INFO:
Calories 192
Calories from Fat 33%
Fat 7g
Saturated Fat 3g
Cholesterol 109mg
Sodium 230mg
Carbohydrates 6g
Dietary Fiber 1g
Total Sugars 2g
Protein 27g
Dietary Exchanges:
1/2 starch, 3 lean meat

CHICKEN BURGERS

  D

A nice tasty change to beef burgers — try them, they're so good.

Makes 5 chicken burgers

1 pound ground chicken breast

1/2 cup chopped green bell pepper

1/2 teaspoon minced garlic

1/2 cup chopped green onions

1 egg

1 tablespoon light mayonnaise

1 tablespoon Dijon mustard

1/2 cup breadcrumbs (seasoned or Italian)

1 In large skillet, cook chicken, green pepper and garlic until chicken is done. Add green onions.

2 In small bowl, whisk together egg, mayonnaise and Dijon; add to chicken mixture with bread crumbs. Season to taste. Shape chicken mixture into 5 patties. Cover and chill 15 minutes.

3 In large nonstick skillet coated with nonstick cooking spray, cook patties several minutes on each side.

NUTRITIONAL INFO:
Calories 182
Calories from Fat 24%
Fat 5g
Saturated Fat 1g
Cholesterol 96mg
Sodium 375mg
Carbohydrates 11g
Dietary Fiber 1g
Total Sugars 2g
Protein 23g
Dietary Exchanges:
1/2 starch,
2 1/2 lean meat

SNAPPY SALMON BURGERS

Fresh salmon makes all the difference with these sensationally delicious burgers full of snap and pop!

Makes 8 salmon burgers

2 pounds fresh salmon fillets, skinned

1/2 cup chopped green onions

1/2 teaspoon minced garlic

2 tablespoons lemon juice

1/2 teaspoon dried dill weed leaves

Salt and pepper to taste

1 egg

1 egg white

2 cups crisp rice cereal

1 With knife or food processor, chop salmon into small pieces.

2 In large bowl, mix together salmon, green onions, garlic, lemon juice, dill and season to taste.

3 In another bowl, whisk together egg and egg white and add to salmon mixture.

4 Using your hands, gently mix salmon mixture with cereal (mixture will be loose). Form mixture into burgers.

5 Heat large nonstick skillet coated with nonstick cooking spray over medium heat. Cook 3-4 minutes on each side or until golden brown.

D

NUTRITIONAL INFO:

Calories 188

Calories from Fat 29%

Fat 6g

Saturated Fat 1g

Cholesterol 76mg

Sodium 142mg

Carbohydrates 7g

Dietary Fiber 0g

Total Sugars 1g

Protein 25g

Dietary Exchanges:
1/2 starch, 3 lean meat

TERRIFIC TIP

Salmon patties may be made ahead of time and refrigerated until ready to cook. If grilling, place salmon patties in freezer about 20-30 minutes and they will hold together better.

Serve with your favorite condiments.

BBQ SHRIMP TACOS

Two of my favorites, BBQ shrimp and tacos, in one marvelous recipe.

Makes 4 servings

1 pound medium shrimp, peeled

1 tablespoon olive oil

2 tablespoons minced garlic

3 tablespoons Worcestershire sauce

1 bunch green onions, chopped

1 teaspoon dried basil leaves

1 tablespoon chili powder

2 tablespoons lemon juice

1/4 cup barbecue sauce

1 cup chopped tomatoes

1/4 cup chopped red onion

Salt and pepper to taste

4 flour tortillas, warmed

TERRIFIC TIP

Peeled shrimp may be bought fresh or frozen. If frozen, defrost first.

Garnish with avocado.

1 In bowl or resealable plastic bag, coat shrimp with olive oil. Add all ingredients except tomatoes, onion, and tortillas. Marinate 1-2 hours, time permitting.

2 In large nonstick skillet coated with nonstick cooking spray, add shrimp (discarding extra marinade). Sauté shrimp until done.

3 In small bowl, combine tomatoes and onion. Season to taste. Make tacos with tortillas, shrimp, and tomato mixture.

PORK TACOS *with* PINEAPPLE SLAW

Sizzling sensation. Southwestern pork chops with a refreshing slaw.

Makes 10 (1-taco) servings

1 (8-ounce) can crushed pineapple, drained, saving juice

1/2 cup nonfat Greek plain yogurt

2 teaspoons chili powder

1 teaspoon cumin

2 tablespoons lime juice

Salt and pepper to taste

2 pounds pork chops, about 1/2-inch thick, trimmed of fat

4 cups cole slaw mix

1 bunch green onions, chopped

1 (4-ounce) can chopped green chilies, drained

10 flour tortillas, warmed

1 In small bowl, combine pineapple juice (set crushed pineapple aside), yogurt, chili powder, cumin, and lime juice. Season to taste.

2 Remove 2/3 cup yogurt mixture and place in plastic bag or dish to marinate pork chops. Refrigerate 10-30 minutes. Set aside remaining yogurt mixture.

3 In large nonstick skillet coated with nonstick cooking spray, cook pork chops (discard marinade) over medium-high heat, browning on each side or until done. Slice into strips.

4 Combine reserved crushed pineapple, cole slaw, green onions, chilies and remaining reserved yogurt mixture. Fill tortillas with pork slices and top with slaw.

D

NUTRITIONAL INFO:

Calories 243

Calories from Fat 28%

Fat 7g

Saturated Fat 2g

Cholesterol 53mg

Sodium 385mg

Carbohydrates 22g

Dietary Fiber 3g

Total Sugars 5g

Protein 21g

Dietary Exchanges:
1 starch, 1/2 fruit,
2 1/2 lean meat

TERRIFIC TIP

To heat tortillas in microwave, cover with damp paper towel 30 seconds or until heated.

FISH TACOS *with* SOUTHWESTERN COLE SLAW

Spicy fish and fabulous cool cole slaw — easy and perfect pairing.

Makes 6 fish tacos

D

NUTRITIONAL INFO:
Calories 209
Calories from Fat 19%
Fat 4g
Saturated Fat 2g
Cholesterol 57mg
Sodium 353mg
Carbohydrates 16g
Dietary Fiber 1g
Total Sugars 1g
Protein 26g
Dietary Exchanges:
1 starch, 3 lean meat

1 1/2 pounds tilapia filets (or fish of choice)

1/2 teaspoon chili powder

Salt and pepper to taste

6 flour tortillas (or corn tortillas)

Southwestern Cole slaw (recipe follows)

1 Preheat broiler. Season fish with chili powder and season to taste. Broil 4-6 minutes per 1/2–inch thickness or until fish flakes with fork. Fish may be grilled or pan sautéed also.

2 Fill each tortilla with fish and Southwestern Cole Slaw (see recipe).

3 Warm tortillas according to package directions or heat in microwave about 30 seconds covered with damp paper towel. Serve with cole slaw or condiments of choice

SOUTHWESTERN COLE SLAW

Serve extra slaw with burgers.

Makes 12 (1/2-cup) servings

 D

NUTRITIONAL INFO:
Calories 76
Calories from Fat 35%
Fat 3g
Saturated Fat 0g
Cholesterol 0mg
Sodium 173mg
Carbohydrates 10g
Dietary Fiber 3g
Total Sugars 4g
Protein 3g
Dietary Exchanges:
1/2 starch, 1/2 fat

1 (10-ounce) bag angel hair or classic cole slaw (about 5 cups)

1 cup chopped green onions

2-3 tablespoons chopped jalapeños (found in jar)

1/2 cup chopped tomatoes

1 (11-ounce) can Mexican style corn, drained

3/4 cup nonfat plain Greek yogurt

1 tablespoon light mayonnaise

2 tablespoons seasoned rice vinegar

1 avocado, chopped and drizzled with lime juice

1 In large bowl, combine cole slaw, green onions, jalapeños, tomatoes, and corn.

2 In small bowl, mix yogurt, mayonnaise, and vinegar. Toss with slaw. Season to taste and fold in avocados.

DOUBLE STUFFED POTATOES

Create a restaurant favorite in your own kitchen easier than you think! Scooping out the potatoes is easy so give it a try.

Makes 4 double stuffed potatoes

2 medium baking potatoes

1/4 cup skim milk

1/4 cup nonfat plain yogurt

Salt and pepper to taste

1/3 cup chopped green onions

4 center cut bacon slices, cooked crispy, cut into small pieces

2/3 cup shredded reduced-fat sharp Cheddar cheese

1 Preheat oven 400°F.

2 Wash potatoes well, and dry thoroughly. Place potatoes directly on oven rack, bake 1 hour or until soft when squeezed. When done, cut each potato in half lengthwise. Scoop out inside, leaving a thin shell.

3 In large bowl, mash potato pulp (with potato masher or mixer) until no lumps remain. Add milk and yogurt, mixing well. Season to taste. Stir in green onions, bacon, and cheese, combining well. Spoon mixture into shells.

4 Lower oven 350°F, bake 15-20 minutes or until cheese is melted and potatoes are hot.

NUTRITIONAL INFO:

Calories 180

Calories from Fat 27%

Fat 5g

Saturated Fat 3g

Cholesterol 18mg

Sodium 283mg

Carbohydrates 22g

Dietary Fiber 2g

Total Sugars 3g

Protein 11g

Dietary Exchanges:
1 1/2 starch,
1 lean meat

TERRIFIC TIP

I always make extra stuffed potatoes to keep in the freezer.

SOUTHWESTERN STUFFED POTATOES

With a few extra ingredients, give your potatoes a southwestern spin. Make a bunch and freeze for a quick lunch.

Makes 6 servings

3 medium baking potatoes

1 tablespoon butter

2 tablespoons skim milk

1/2 cup nonfat plain yogurt

1 1/2 cups frozen corn, thawed

1 (4-ounce) can diced green chiles, optional

4 green onions, chopped

1 cup shredded reduced-fat Cheddar cheese

1 Preheat oven 400°F.

2 Wash potatoes well, and dry thoroughly. Place potatoes directly on oven rack, bake 1 hour or until soft when squeezed. When done, cut each potato in half lengthwise. Scoop out inside, leaving a thin shell.

3 In large bowl, mash potato pulp (with potato masher or mixer) until no lumps remain. Add butter, milk, and yogurt, mixing well. Stir in corn, green chiles, green onions, and cheese, combining well. Spoon mixture into shells.

4 Lower oven 350°F, bake 20 minutes or until cheese is melted and potatoes are hot.

NUTRITIONAL INFO:

Calories 208

Calories from Fat 22%

Fat 5g

Saturated Fat 3g

Cholesterol 16mg

Sodium 159mg

Carbohydrates 33g

Dietary Fiber 3g

Total Sugars 5g

Protein 10g

Dietary Exchanges:
2 starch, 1 lean meat

TERRIFIC TIP

*Sometimes I add
chopped cilantro.*

SWEET POTATO SKINS

This all-American favorite gets a deliciously healthy spin with fiber-rich sweet potatoes and healthier ingredients ideal for any appetizer or snack.

Makes 12 potato skins

6 medium sweet potatoes

4 slices turkey bacon, cooked and crumbled

1/2 cup chopped green onions

2/3 cup reduced-fat shredded Cheddar cheese

1 Wash potatoes well, and dry thoroughly. Microwave on high 8-10 minutes depending on size (or in 425°F oven bake 50-60 minutes). When potatoes cool to handle, cut in half lengthwise; scoop out pulp, leaving a 1/4-inch shell (save pulp for another use). Cut potato skins in half width-wise.

2 Place potato skins on baking sheet lined with foil. Coat skins with nonstick cooking spray.

3 Bake 475°F for 5-7 minutes; turn and coat skins on other side with nonstick cooking spray. Bake until crisp, 3-5 minutes more.

4 In small bowl, mix together bacon, green onions, and cheese. Sprinkle mixture inside skins. Bake 2 minutes longer or until cheese is melted.

 D

NUTRITIONAL INFO:

Calories 79

Calories from Fat 25%

Fat 2g

Saturated Fat 1g

Cholesterol 7mg

Sodium 155mg

Carbohydrates 11g

Dietary Fiber 2g

Total Sugars 2g

Protein 4g

Dietary Exchanges:
1 starch, 1/2 lean meat

TERRIFIC TIP

With the extra potato pulp, make mashed sweet potatoes by mixing in skim milk, sour cream, salt and pepper and maybe a dash of cinnamon.

SMASHED POTATO MOUNDS

 D

NUTRITIONAL INFO:

Calories 54

Calories from Fat 32%

Fat 2g

Saturated Fat 0g

Cholesterol 0mg

Sodium 3mg

Carbohydrates 8g

Dietary Fiber 1g

Total Sugars 0g

Protein 1g

Dietary Exchanges:
1/2 starch, 1/2 fat

TERRIFIC TIP

To serve, set up the condiments and let everyone sprinkle their condiment of choice on these yummy potatoes.

A cross between potato skins and mashed potatoes, these versatile delectable bites make a fun side, snack or pick-up. With or without condiments, these potatoes are tops on my list.

Makes 14 (3-mound) servings

1 (24-ounce) bag "1 bite" potatoes or small round potatoes

2 tablespoons olive oil

Salt and pepper to taste

Condiments of choice: cheese, green onions, sour cream, Italian seasoning, optional

1 In large pot, bring potatoes covered with water to a boil. Cook about 15- 20minutes depending on size of potatoes or until fork-tender. Drain potatoes.

2 Preheat oven 450°F. Coat baking pan with nonstick cooking spray.

3 Spread cooked potatoes on prepared baking sheet, leaving room between potatoes. With fork, gently press down each potato until it slightly mashes, rotate fork and mash potato again from other direction. Brush tops of each mashed potato mound with olive oil.

4 Salt and pepper to taste. Bake 20-25 minutes or until golden brown. Remove from oven and sprinkle with cheese or choice of condiments, if desired.

BBQ CHICKEN PIZZA

Nothing beats this all-time easy favorite.

Makes 8 servings

1 pound boneless, skinless chicken breasts, cut into small pieces

Salt and pepper to taste

2 tablespoons plus 3/4 cup barbecue sauce, divided

1 (10-13.8-ounce) can refrigerated pizza crust or Boboli crust

1 1/2 cups shredded part-skim mozzarella cheese or reduced-fat Cheddar cheese (or combination)

1 small red onion, thinly sliced

1/4 cup chopped green onions

1 Preheat oven 425°F.

2 In large nonstick skillet, season chicken to taste and stir-fry over medium heat until done. Remove to bowl and toss with 2 tablespoons barbecue sauce.

3 Coat nonstick pizza pan with nonstick cooking spray. Unroll crust and place in pan; starting at center, press out with hands. Spread pizza crust with remaining 3/4 cup sauce. Sprinkle evenly with cheese, red onion slices, chicken and green onions.

4 Bake 8-10 minutes or until light golden brown.

NUTRITIONAL INFO:

Calories 271

Calories from Fat 23%

Fat 7g

Saturated Fat 3g

Cholesterol 50mg

Sodium 569mg

Carbohydrates 28g

Dietary Fiber 1g

Total Sugars 12g

Protein 21g

Dietary Exchanges:
1 starch,
1 other carbohydrate,
2 1/2 lean meat

TERRIFIC TIP

Great option to use leftover or rostisserie chicken for a quick meal.

MEXICAN MEATY PIZZA

Scrumptious and simple, I keep these ingredients on hand to whip up a meal or to serve for unexpected company.

Makes 12 slices or 48 pick-up pieces

1/2 pound ground sirloin

1 teaspoon chili powder

1 teaspoon ground cumin

2 (8-ounce) cans reduced-fat crescent rolls

2/3 cup salsa

1 1/4 cups reduced-fat Mexican blend cheese

1/2 cup chopped tomatoes

4 green onions, chopped

1 Preheat oven 375°F. Cover 11x15x2-inch baking pan with foil. Coat with nonstick cooking spray.

2 In nonstick pan, cook meat until done; drain any excess liquid. Add chili powder and cumin.

3 Unroll crescent rolls into rectangles and place in prepared pan. Press rolls sealing together over bottom and 1/2 inch up sides to form crust. Bake 11-13 minutes or just until golden brown.

4 Remove from oven and cover evenly with salsa, sprinkle with cheese, tomatoes, and green onions. Return to oven 3-6 more minutes or until cheese is melted.

NUTRITIONAL INFO:

Calories 190

Calories from Fat 43%

Fat 9g

Saturated Fat 4g

Cholesterol 18mg

Sodium 460mg

Carbohydrates 19g

Dietary Fiber 1g

Total Sugars 4g

Protein 10g

Dietary Exchanges:
1 starch, 1 lean meat, 1 fat

TERRIFIC TIP

For a variation you can put a thin layer of refried beans (heat in microwave to soften) instead of salsa.

GARDEN PIZZA

An effortless pizza crust you pat down, sprinkle with Italian seasoning, top with fresh ingredients and cheese; pop in the oven and you have a superb pizza in minutes.

Makes 8 servings

1 1/2 cups biscuit baking mix

1/3 cup very hot water

2 tablespoons olive oil

2 teaspoons dried basil leaves

1 teaspoon dried oregano leaves

1 cup baby spinach

1/3 cup chopped tomatoes

1/2 cup chopped red onion

1 cup part-skim shredded mozzarella cheese

1 Heat oven 450ºF. Coat pizza pan with nonstick cooking spray.

2 In bowl, stir together baking mix and hot water; beat until soft dough forms. Press dough in pizza pan. Spread olive oil on crust, and sprinkle with basil and oregano. Top with remaining ingredients.

3 Bake 10-12 minutes or until crust is golden brown and cheese is bubbly.

NUTRITIONAL INFO:

Calories 164

Calories from Fat 46%

Fat 9g

Saturated Fat 3g

Cholesterol 9mg

Sodium 370mg

Carbohydrates 17g

Dietary Fiber 1g

Total Sugars 1g

Protein 5g

Dietary Exchanges:
1 starch, 1/2 lean meat, 1 fat

TERRIFIC TIP

You can use a prepared pizza crust, if desired, but this crust takes minutes to make.

Cheesy Burger Dip (pg 132)

6

FIX IT FAST

MEDITERRANEAN LAYERED SPREAD

Doesn't get much better than this stunning and stupendous Greek layered spread; my go-to make-ahead guaranteed hit.

Makes 14 servings

1 (8-ounce) package reduced-fat cream cheese

1/2 cup nonfat plain Greek yogurt

1 teaspoon dried oregano leaves

1/2 teaspoon minced garlic

2 teaspoons lemon juice

Salt and pepper to taste

1 1/2 cups roasted red pepper hummus

1 cup chopped tomatoes

1 cup chopped cucumber

1/3 cup chopped green onions

1/4 cup crumbled reduced-fat feta cheese

3 tablespoons sliced Kalamata or black olives

1 In bowl, blend together cream cheese, yogurt, oregano, garlic, lemon juice and season to taste. Spread on large round serving plate.

2 Carefully spread hummus over cream cheese. Sprinkle evenly with remaining ingredients, refrigerate until serving time.

NUTRITIONAL INFO:

Calories 100

Calories from Fat 59%

Fat 7g

Saturated Fat 3g

Cholesterol 13mg

Sodium 260mg

Carbohydrates 6g

Dietary Fiber 1g

Total Sugars 2g

Protein 4g

Dietary Exchanges:
1/2 starch,
1/2 lean meat, 1 fat

TERRIFIC TIP

Serve with pita chips or sliced vegetables.

You can easily make your own pita chips by cutting pitas into 6 triangles and baking 5-7 minutes at 375°F.

PARMESAN PITA PICK-UPS

These crispy Italian seasoned pitas (like chips) are fantastic served warm or room temperature. Make the filling ahead of time, refrigerate and put together for a great last minute appetizer or snack.

Makes 15 (4-triangle) servings

1/2 cup light mayonnaise

1/4 cup nonfat plain yogurt

3/4 cup grated Parmesan cheese

1 teaspoon dried basil leaves

1 teaspoon dried oregano leaves

1 teaspoon lemon juice

5 whole pita breads (whole wheat)

1 Preheat oven 350°F. Coat baking pan with nonstick cooking spray.

2 In small bowl, mix together all ingredients except pita bread.

3 Split pita bread in half and cut each whole into six triangles (each pita makes 12 triangles). Spread each triangle with about 1/2 teaspoon mixture. Bake 8-10 minutes or until crispy.

 D

NUTRITIONAL INFO:

Calories 92

Calories from Fat 33%

Fat 4g

Saturated Fat 1g

Cholesterol 0mg

Sodium 6mg

Carbohydrates 12g

Dietary Fiber 1g

Total Sugars 1g

Protein 4g

Dietary Exchanges:
1 starch, 1/2 fat

TERRIFIC TIP

Use kitchen scissors to easily cut pitas.

Italian seasoning blend may be substituted for basil and oregano.

CHEESY BURGER DIP

NUTRITIONAL INFO:

Calories 72

Calories from Fat 41%

Fat 3g

Saturated Fat 2g

Cholesterol 19mg

Sodium 176mg

Carbohydrates 2g

Dietary Fiber 0g

Total Sugars 1g

Protein 8g

Dietary Exchanges:
1 lean meat

TERRIFIC TIP

Turn leftover dip into a delicious meal tossed with pasta or served over rice.

Try serving in a small slow cooker to keep it warm.

Satisfying and simple four ingredient quick-fix dip. Serve with chips of choice.

Makes 20 (1/4-cup) servings

1 pound ground sirloin

1/2 pound sliced mushrooms

1 (16-ounce) jar salsa

1 (8-ounce) package shredded reduced-fat Mexican-blend cheese

1 In nonstick pot, cook meat and mushrooms over medium heat 5–7 minutes, until meat is well browned. Drain any excess fat.

2 Add salsa and cheese, stirring over medium heat until cheese is melted.

TOMATO BASIL SOUP

A simple soup but this time fresh basil is a must! Adjust the basil according to preference.

Makes 4 (1-cup) servings

1 tablespoon olive oil

1/3 cup finely chopped onion

1 teaspoon minced garlic

1 (28-ounce) can chopped tomatoes, with juice

2 tablespoons sun-dried tomatoes (found in jar), drained

2 cups fat-free vegetable or chicken broth

1 cup loosely packed chopped fresh basil

Salt and pepper to taste

1/2 cup skim milk

1/4 cup Italian blend shredded cheese, optional

1. In large nonstick pot, heat oil and sauté onion and garlic over medium heat until tender, about 5 minutes.

2. Add tomatoes and juice, sun-dried tomatoes, and broth. Bring to boil, reduce heat and cook until soup is thickened, about 20 minutes.

3. Stir in the basil and season to taste. Transfer to a food processor and blend until very smooth. Return to pot and stir in milk and cheese, if desired.

NUTRITIONAL INFO:

Calories 107

Calories from Fat 35%

Fat 4g

Saturated Fat 1g

Cholesterol 1mg

Sodium 510mg

Carbohydrates 13g

Dietary Fiber 2g

Total Sugars 8g

Protein 4g

Dietary Exchanges:
2 vegetable, 1 fat

TERRIFIC TIP

Fresh basil is available in any grocery in the produce section. Of course, dried basil may be used (about 1 tablespoon) but fresh does make a difference.

ROASTED SALMON & BROCCOLI SALAD

D

TERRIFIC TIP

Have leftover salmon from the night before, turn into this main dish salad.

Depending on thickness of salmon, roast about 10 minutes per inch.

Roasting, one-step cooking, boosts the flavor of the salmon and broccoli — makes an amazing simple salad.

Makes 5 (1-cup) servings

1 (16-ounce) salmon fillet

4 cups broccoli florets

2 teaspoons olive oil

Salt and pepper to taste

1 cup grape tomatoes, halved

1/3 cup chopped red onion

2 cups chopped cucumber

2 tablespoons chopped fresh basil or 2 teaspoons dried basil leaves

Vinaigrette (recipe follows)

4 cups assorted mixed salad greens

1. Preheat oven 400°F. Cover baking sheet with foil.

2. Place salmon on one side of pan and broccoli on other side. Toss broccoli with olive oil and season to taste. Roast 15-20 minutes, or until salmon is done. Cool salmon and flake with fork.

3. In large bowl, combine flaked salmon, roasted broccoli, tomatoes, onion, cucumber and basil. Toss with Vinaigrette (see recipe) and serve over mixed greens.

VINAIGRETTE

1 tablespoon olive oil

1/4 cup seasoned rice or white vinegar

1 tablespoon lemon juice

1 teaspoon Dijon mustard

1. In small bowl, whisk together all ingredients.

Roasted Salmon & Broccoli Salad (pg 134)

GREAT GREEK COUSCOUS

 D

Couscous provides an easy start for fresh summer ingredients making a quick toss–together light summer specialty salad. Give couscous a try, you won't believe how easy it is to prepare.

Makes 6 (1-cup) servings

2 cups water

1 1/2 cups Israeli couscous or couscous

1 cup chopped tomato

1 bunch green onions, chopped

1 cup packed baby spinach

1/3 cup sliced Kalamata olives

1/4 cup reduced-fat feta cheese

3 tablespoons chopped fresh basil or 1 tablespoon dried basil leaves

2 tablespoons vinegar

1 In medium pot, bring water to boil. Add couscous and follow directions on couscous container.

2 Transfer to large bowl and add all other ingredients, tossing carefully. Season to taste.

NUTRITIONAL INFO:

Calories 224

Calories from Fat 15%

Fat 4g

Saturated Fat 1g

Cholesterol 2mg

Sodium 318mg

Carbohydrates 40g

Dietary Fiber 4g

Total Sugars 3g

Protein 7g

Dietary Exchanges:
2 1/2 starch,
1 vegetable, 1/2 fat

TERRIFIC TIP

I like the Israeli couscous as it is a bigger grain but any couscous may be used. Couscous is a type of coarsely ground semolina pasta, that can be found in the pasta section of the grocery.

MARVELOUS MARINARA SAUCE

A basic marinara sauce with options. Serve with pasta and sprinkle with Parmesan cheese.

Makes 4 (1-cup) servings

2 teaspoons olive oil

1/3 cup chopped onion

1 teaspoon minced garlic

1/4 teaspoon hot pepper flakes

1/4 cup fat-free vegetable or chicken broth

1 (28-ounce) can diced tomatoes

1 teaspoon dried oregano leaves

1 teaspoon dried basil leaves

1 In large nonstick skillet, heat oil and sauté onion, garlic and pepper flakes 4 minutes or until onion is tender. Add broth and cook until liquid has evaporated, about 3 minutes.

2 Add tomatoes to skillet, bring to boil, lower heat and cook 5 minutes.

3 Add oregano and basil, cook on medium heat 10 minutes, stirring frequently.

NUTRITIONAL INFO:

Calories 69

Calories from Fat 28%

Fat 2g

Saturated Fat 0g

Cholesterol 0mg

Sodium 374mg

Carbohydrates 11g

Dietary Fiber 4g

Total Sugars 7g

Protein 2g

Dietary Exchanges:
2 vegetable, 1/2 fat

TERRIFIC TIP

Try adding capers or olives for an added punch of flavor to this marvelous dish if that is your thing.... it is mine!

ONE DISH CHICKEN ORZO

 D

NUTRITIONAL INFO:

Calories 332

Calories from Fat 20%

Fat 7g

Saturated Fat 1g

Cholesterol 73mg

Sodium 559mg

Carbohydrates 34g

Dietary Fiber 2g

Total Sugars 2g

Protein 30g

Dietary Exchanges:
2 starch, 3 lean meat

TERRIFIC TIP

Orzo is a rice shaped pasta found in the pasta aisle.

Put chicken between sheets of waxed paper and pound.

On a busy night, here's your solution for a light delicious chicken dinner that will perk up your palate.

Makes 4 servings

4 (4-5-ounce) chicken breasts, pounded thin

1 tablespoon all-purpose flour

Pepper to taste

1 tablespoon olive oil

1 (14 1/2-ounce) can fat-free chicken broth

2 tablespoons lemon juice

1 teaspoon dried oregano leaves

2 tablespoons sliced Kalamata olives, optional

1 cup orzo

1/3 cup chopped green onions

1. Coat chicken breasts with flour and season with pepper.

2. In large nonstick skillet, heat oil and cook chicken until browned on both sides. Add broth, lemon juice, oregano and olives, if desired. Stir in orzo.

3. Bring to boil, lower heat, cover and cook 20-25 minutes or until chicken is tender and orzo is done (broth absorbed). Stir in green onions and cook one minute.

CHICKEN SCALLOPINI

A last minute meal with surprisingly sensational flavors.

Makes 4 servings

1/4 cup all-purpose flour

1/2 teaspoon garlic powder

Pepper to taste

1 1/4 pounds boneless, skinless chicken breasts, pounded thin (about four)

2 tablespoons olive oil

1 1/4 cups fat-free chicken broth

2 tablespoons lemon juice

1 tablespoon chopped parsley

1 In shallow bowl, combine flour, garlic powder, and pepper. Coat chicken with flour mixture.

2 In large nonstick skillet coated with nonstick cooking spray, heat oil. Add chicken breasts, and cook until lightly browned, about 4 minutes each side.

3 Add broth, bring to boil, reduce heat, cover, and simmer until chicken is tender, 15–20 minutes. Add lemon juice and sprinkle with parsley before serving.

 D

NUTRITIONAL INFO:
Calories 258
Calories from Fat 38%
Fat 11g
Saturated Fat 2g
Cholesterol 91mg
Sodium 287mg
Carbohydrates 7g
Dietary Fiber 1g
Total Sugars 0g
Protein 32g
Dietary Exchanges:
1/2 starch, 4 lean meat

TERRIFIC TIP

You can buy thin chicken breasts in the grocery instead of pounding them.

SIMPLE SURPRISE FISH

D

For a quick fish dinner, try this snappy light fish that pops with flavor — with no clean-up.

Makes 4 servings

1 (14 1/2-ounce) can fire-roasted tomatoes, well drained

2 tablespoons chopped onion

1 tablespoon finely chopped fresh ginger

1 teaspoon minced garlic

1 teaspoon finely chopped jalapeño peppers (jarred)

Salt and pepper to taste

4 (4-6 ounce) fish fillets

1 Preheat oven 500°F. Tear off four sheets of aluminum foil to hold fish or can use baking bag.

2 In small bowl, combine tomatoes, onion, ginger, garlic, and jalapeño. Set aside.

3 Season fish to taste. Place fish fillet on each piece of foil. Top each fillet with heaping 1/4 cup tomato mixture. Seal packets tightly, folding the edges over and place on baking sheet.

4 Bake 12 minutes or until fish is cooked through. Serve in foil pouch.

TERRIFIC TIP

No fresh ginger? Use 1 teaspoon ground ginger.

BLACKENED FISH

Restaurant friendly recipe with no fuss and lots of flavor.

Makes 4 servings

2 tablespoons paprika

1 teaspoon chili powder

1/2 teaspoon dried thyme leaves

1 teaspoon garlic powder

1 teaspoon pepper

1/2 teaspoon salt

1 1/2 pounds fish fillets

2 tablespoons olive oil

1 In small bowl or plastic bag, combine all ingredients, except fish and oil. Coat both sides of fish with spice mixture.

2 In large nonstick skillet, heat oil over medium-high heat. Place fish in hot pan and cook 2-3 minutes on each side until fish flakes with fork.

D

NUTRITIONAL INFO:

Calories 232

Calories from Fat 36%

Fat 9g

Saturated Fat 1g

Cholesterol 63mg

Sodium 395mg

Carbohydrates 3g

Dietary Fiber 2g

Total Sugars 0g

Protein 34g

Dietary Exchanges:
4 1/2 lean meat

TERRIFIC TIP

Fish is done when center is white and opaque — no longer translucent.

Any fresh fish may be used such as grouper, halibut, tilapia, trout or catfish.

SALMON *with* DILL DIJON SAUCE

D

TERRIFIC TIP

Instead of one large piece of salmon, you can use individual pieces for individual servings.

I have served this as an appetizer and a main dish at cocktail parties — either way guests were so impressed.

Salmon with easy preparation and a special presentation.

Makes 6 servings

1 (2-pound) fresh salmon fillet

1 cup dry white wine

Salt and pepper to taste

1/3 cup spicy or creole mustard

1/4 cup light brown sugar

Dill Dijon Sauce (recipe follows)

1. Preheat oven 350°F. Line baking sheet with foil.

2. Lay salmon on prepared pan. Pour wine over salmon and season to taste. Bake 20-25 minutes or until almost done.

3. Turn oven to broil. In bowl, mix together mustard and brown sugar; spread on top salmon. Return salmon to oven; broil until topping is brown and bubbling, about 3 minutes — watch carefully. Serve with Dill Dijon Sauce (see recipe).

DILL DIJON SAUCE

1 cup nonfat plain yogurt

1 1/2 tablespoons white vinegar

1 1/2 tablespoons Dijon mustard

3 tablespoons light brown sugar

2 teaspoons dried dill weed leaves

1. In small bowl, mix together all ingredients. Refrigerate.

ASIAN SHRIMP *with* ORANGE DIPPING SAUCE

Quick to cook flavorful shrimp is good alone or top a salad.

Makes 4 servings

1 pound medium-large peeled shrimp

2 tablespoons low-sodium soy sauce

2 tablespoons lemon juice

1 teaspoon minced fresh ginger

1 teaspoon cumin

1 tablespoon canola or sesame oil

Orange Dipping Sauce (recipe follows)

1 Combine all ingredients except oil in plastic bag and refrigerate until ready to cook.

2 Grill shrimp or cook in large nonstick skillet in heated oil 3-5 minutes on each side, or until done (discard marinade). Serve with Orange Dipping Sauce (see recipe).

ORANGE DIPPING SAUCE

1/2 cup orange marmalade

1/4 cup hoisin sauce

2 tablespoons sweet chili sauce

1/2 teaspoon grated fresh ginger

1 Combine all ingredients together in bowl.

D

NUTRITIONAL INFO:

Calories 218

Calories from Fat 5%

Fat 1g

Saturated Fat 0g

Cholesterol 143mg

Sodium 521mg

Carbohydrates 37g

Dietary Fiber 0g

Total Sugars 32g

Protein 16g

Dietary Exchanges:
2 1/2 other carbohydrate,
2 1/2 lean meat

TERRIFIC TIP

Orange Dipping Sauce is a sweet sauce with a bit of a bite as it is good with shrimp, chicken, or your favorite meat.

LEMON HERB SHRIMP

D

Pick up a loaf of French bread to dip into the fabulous sauce with the terrific tasting shrimp. Serve with angel hair pasta for a super meal.

Makes 6-8 servings

NUTRITIONAL INFO:
Calories 206
Calories from Fat 65%
Fat 15g
Saturated Fat 2g
Cholesterol 143mg
Sodium 257mg
Carbohydrates 3g
Dietary Fiber 1g
Total Sugars 0g
Protein 16g
Dietary Exchanges:
2 lean meat, 2 fat

1/2 cup olive oil
2 teaspoons dried oregano leaves
2 teaspoons dried thyme leaves
1/2 cup chopped green onion
2 teaspoons grated lemon rind
1/4 cup lemon juice
Salt and pepper
2 pounds medium shrimp, peeled

1 Combine all ingredients except shrimp in resealable plastic bag. Add shrimp, tossing to coat. Refrigerate one hour, time permitting.

2 Preheat oven 450°F. Place shrimp and marinade on foil lined baking pan. Bake 10 minutes (depending on shrimp size) or until shrimp are done and marinade bubbling. Serve shrimp with sauce.

TERRIFIC TIP

Don't have lemon rind, just leave it out. For lemon rind, finely grate or zest the outside of the lemon to get only lemon peel.

SHRIMP & ARTICHOKE PASTA DISH

A perfect pairing of shrimp, artichokes, and herbs in a simple rich tasting sauce resembling Alfredo. Cooking the pasta takes the most time with this stress-free recipe.

Makes 6 (1-cup) servings

8 ounces linguine

6 ounces reduced-fat cream cheese

1/2 cup skim milk

1 tablespoon Worcestershire sauce

2 tablespoons lemon juice

1 tablespoon dried dill weed leaves, oregano or herb of choice

1 pound medium peeled shrimp

1 (14-ounce) can artichokes, drained and quartered

1 bunch green onions, chopped

1 Cook pasta according to package directions, drain and return to pot.

2 While pasta is cooking, in small microwave-safe bowl, combine cream cheese and milk; microwave 1 minute. Stir and continue to microwave 30 seconds or until creamy. Add Worcestershire sauce, lemon juice and herbs.

3 In small nonstick skillet coated with nonstick cooking spray, cook shrimp about 5 minutes or until done, turning pink.

4 In pot with pasta, add shrimp, cream cheese sauce, artichokes and green onions, tossing together.

NUTRITIONAL INFO:

Calories 303

Calories from Fat 23%

Fat 7g

Saturated Fat 4g

Cholesterol 116mg

Sodium 454mg

Carbohydrates 37g

Dietary Fiber 3g

Total Sugars 5g

Protein 20g

Dietary Exchanges:
2 starch, 1 vegetable, 2 lean meat

TERRIFIC TIP

I make this dish with dill, but any herb of choice will go with the rich tasting sauce.

THAI BEEF LETTUCE WRAPS

NUTRITIONAL INFO:

Calories 205

Calories from Fat 31%

Fat 7g

Saturated Fat 3g

Cholesterol 62mg

Sodium 202mg

Carbohydrates 10g

Dietary Fiber 2g

Total Sugars 6g

Protein 25g

Dietary Exchanges:
1 vegetable, 1/2 other carbohydrate,
3 lean meat

A tangy, spicy meat mixture with toasted sesame seeds wrapped up in lettuce leaves for a simple from scratch meal.

Makes 4 (1/2-cup) servings

1 pound ground sirloin

1 cup chopped onion

1/2 teaspoon minced garlic

1/2 teaspoon crushed red pepper flakes

3 tablespoons hoisin sauce

1 teaspoon grated fresh ginger or 1/4 teaspoon ground ginger

1 tablespoon sesame seeds, toasted

1 tablespoon seasoned rice vinegar

1/2 cup chopped green onions

Boston or red tip lettuce leaves

1. In large nonstick skillet, cook meat, onion, and garlic over medium heat 7 minutes, or until done. Drain excess grease.

2. Stir in pepper flakes, hoisin sauce, ginger, sesame seeds, vinegar, and green onions.

3. Divide mixture on lettuce leaves, wrap to eat.

TERRIFIC TIP

If you cannot find Boston or red tip lettuce, any large lettuce leaf will do, just make sure it is big enough to wrap.

I like to use Butter or Bibb lettuce which is another name for Boston.

EASY MEAT SAUCE

By using a jar of marinara with fresh vegetables, you get an easy homemade meat sauce that's great with any pasta.

Makes 8 (1-cup) servings

1 large onion, chopped

1 medium yellow squash, thinly sliced

1 medium zucchini, thinly sliced

2 pounds ground sirloin

1 tablespoon minced garlic

1 (24-ounce) jar marinara sauce

1 tablespoon dried basil leaves

1 tablespoon dried oregano leaves

Pinch sugar

Salt and pepper to taste

1 In large nonstick skillet coated with nonstick cooking spray, sauté onion, squash, and zucchini about 5 minutes. Add meat and garlic and cook over medium heat until meat is done and vegetables are tender, 5-7 minutes. Drain excess grease.

2 Add marinara, basil, oregano and sugar. Bring to boil, stirring constantly. Reduce heat, and simmer, uncovered, 20 minutes or time permitting. Season to taste.

NUTRITIONAL INFO:

Calories 220
Calories from Fat 31%
Fat 8g
Saturated Fat 3g
Cholesterol 62mg
Sodium 438mg
Carbohydrates 12g
Dietary Fiber 3g
Total Sugars 3g
Protein 27g
Dietary Exchanges:
2 vegetable, 3 lean meat

TERRIFIC TIP

Meat sauce freezes great so freeze in individual zip-top freezer bags to pull out for meals. The squash may be left out, if desired.

SIMPLE SOUTHWESTERN CASSEROLE

NUTRITIONAL INFO:
Calories 257
Calories from Fat 28%
Fat 8g
Saturated Fat 4g
Cholesterol 36mg
Sodium 815mg
Carbohydrates 27g
Dietary Fiber 4g
Total Sugars 5g
Protein 20g
Dietary Exchanges:
1 1/2 starch,
1 vegetable,
2 lean meat

TERRIFIC TIP

Use kitchen scissors to make cutting biscuits easy.

If you have trouble finding enchilada sauce, you can substitute salsa.

Zesty, meaty casserole with a biscuit surprise — you will be amazed at how extraordinarily tasty this simple combination is. This recipe has become so popular in my family.

Makes 9 (1-cup) servings

1 pound ground sirloin

1 onion, chopped

1 (10-ounce) can enchilada sauce

1 (8-ounce) can tomato sauce

1 (15-ounce) can black beans, rinsed and drained

1 cup frozen corn

1 (8-10 count) can reduced-fat refrigerator biscuits

1 cup shredded reduced-fat Mexican blend cheese

1/3 cup chopped green onions

1 Preheat oven 350°F. Coat 13x9x2-inch baking dish with nonstick cooking spray.

2 In large nonstick skillet, cook meat and onion until meat is done; drain excess fat. Add enchilada sauce, tomato sauce, black beans and corn, stirring well. Cut biscuits into fourths and stir into meat mixture.

3 Transfer to prepared pan. Bake 25 minutes. Remove from oven, sprinkle with cheese and green onions. Return to oven and bake 5-7 minutes more or until cheese is melted.

CUBAN STUFFED PORK TENDERLOIN

Perky flavors are packed into this eye-catching tenderloin.
Serve sliced to see the stuffing.

Makes 6 servings

2 (1-pound) pork tenderloins

1 teaspoon minced garlic

2 tablespoons Dijon mustard

1/3 cup chopped parsley

1/3 cup shredded part-skim mozzarella cheese

1/3 cup chopped bread and butter pickles

Pepper to taste

1 Preheat oven 350°F. Cover baking pan with foil.

2 Make a slit down center of each tenderloin, not cutting through (butterfly).

3 Spread inside of both tenderloins with garlic and mustard. Stuff with parsley, cheese and pickles. Fold sides together securing with twine or threading toothpicks to hold together. Season tenderloin with pepper. Bake 40-45 minutes or until meat thermometer registers 160°F.

NUTRITIONAL INFO:
Calories 232
Calories from Fat 33%
Fat 8g
Saturated Fat 3g
Cholesterol 104mg
Sodium 264mg
Carbohydrates 3g
Dietary Fiber 0g
Total Sugars 2g
Protein 34g
Dietary Exchanges:
4 1/2 lean meat

TERRIFIC TIP

Turn leftovers into Cuban quesadillas or sandwiches. In tortilla, layer pork (shred if possible), Swiss cheese, pickle slices and mustard and heat in skillet.

Don't have bread and butter pickles? Use any pickles.

BBQ Shrimp (pg 168)

7

CROCK POT CONVENIENCE

LIGHT & LOADED POTATO SOUP

Starting with hash browns (no peeling potatoes) makes this an incredibly fabulous, yet simple soup.

NUTRITIONAL INFO:

Calories 256

Calories from Fat 2%

Fat 1g

Saturated Fat 0g

Cholesterol 2mg

Sodium 1051mg

Carbohydrates 51g

Dietary Fiber 4g

Total Sugars 10g

Protein 13g

Dietary Exchanges:
3 starch, 1/2 fat free mil

TERRIFIC TIP

I like using Greek yogurt as it is richer and creamer than plain yogurt.

Makes 8 (1-cup) servings

6 cups frozen hash brown potatoes, partially thawed

1 onion, chopped

6 cups fat-free chicken or vegetable broth

1/4 cup all-purpose flour

1 (12-ounce) can evaporated skimmed milk, divided

3/4 cup nonfat plain Greek yogurt

Salt and pepper to taste

Green onions, cheese, turkey bacon, optional toppings

1 In 3 1/2-6-quart slow cooker, insert plastic liner if desired. Mix potatoes, onion, and broth. Cook on LOW 6-8 hours.

2 In small bowl, mix flour into milk; stir into potato mixture. Increase to HIGH. Cover; cook 20-30 minutes or until mixture thickens. Stir in yogurt and season to taste.

3 Serve with green onions, cheese, and bacon, if desired.

SWEET POTATO CHILI

Chop some veggies, open some cans, and toss in the slow cooker for an amazing snappy vegetarian chili with naturally sweet yams and a fiery smoky flavor.

Makes 8 (1-cup) servings

4 cups Louisiana yams, (sweet potatoes), peeled and cut into 2-inch chunks (about 1 3/4 pounds)

1 onion, chopped

1 teaspoon minced garlic

1 (15-ounce) can dark red kidney beans, rinsed and drained

1 red bell pepper, seeded and chopped

1 (14 1/2-ounce) can fire roasted diced tomatoes

2 tablespoons chili powder

1 teaspoon ground cumin

1 1/2 teaspoons paprika

1 cup water or vegetable broth

1/2 cup orange juice or water

1 In 3 1/2-6-quart slow cooker, insert plastic liner if desired, and add all ingredients to pot. Cook on LOW 6-8 hours, or until sweet potatoes are tender.

NUTRITIONAL INFO:

Calories 166

Calories from Fat 3%

Fat 1g

Saturated Fat 0g

Cholesterol 0mg

Sodium 261mg

Carbohydrates 37g

Dietary Fiber 9g

Total Sugars 10g

Protein 6g

Dietary Exchanges:
2 starch, 1 vegetable

TERRIFIC TIP

Make this even easier by cutting up vegetables the night before so are ready to go in morning. Cut slow-cooking vegetables, such as carrots, into small pieces. Cut quick-cooking vegetables, such as sweet peppers into bigger pieces.

Can serve over couscous, polenta, or rice, if desired.

TACO SOUP

Here's my version of a simple and speedy favorite that stands the test of time. If you can open cans, this soup is for you.

Makes 10 (1-cup) servings

1 pound ground sirloin

2 (10-ounce) cans diced tomatoes and green chilies

1 (15-ounce) can black beans, rinsed and drained

1 (15-ounce) can kidney beans, rinsed and drained

1 (15-ounce) can pinto beans, rinsed and drained

2 (11-ounce) cans Mexican style corn, drained

1 (4-ounce) can chopped green chilies, drained

1 (1 1/4-ounce) package taco seasoning mix

1 (1-ounce) package original ranch salad dressing mix

2 cups water

1 In large nonstick skillet, over medium heat, cook meat until done, 5 minutes. Drain any excess grease.

2 In 3 1/2-6-quart slow cooker, insert plastic liner if desired, and add cooked meat and all ingredients to pot. Cook on LOW 6-8 hours, or until sweet potatoes are tender.

NUTRITIONAL INFO:

Calories 317

Calories from Fat 12%

Fat 3g

Saturated Fat 1g

Cholesterol 25mg

Sodium 1406mg

Carbohydrates 37g

Dietary Fiber 8g

Total Sugars 4g

Protein 19g

Dietary Exchanges:
2 1/2 starch, 2 lean meat

TERRIFIC TIP

To reduce the sodium, use reduced-sodium taco seasoning mix and then the recipe will be diabetic friendly!

I added sweet potatoes for a colorful nutritional boost.

EASY ROAST

Intimidated by cooking a roast? Don't be — three ingredients make up a scrumptious sauce. Toss in slow cooker and your work is done for a memorable meal

Makes 8 (6-ounce) servings

1 (4-pound) beef sirloin tip roast, trimmed of excess fat

6 garlic cloves, sliced or garlic powder

Pepper to taste

1 cup light beer

1 (12-ounce) bottle chili sauce

1 envelope onion soup mix

1 Cut slits in roast and stuff pieces of garlic throughout meat. Season meat with pepper.

2 In 3 1/2-6-quart slow cooker, insert plastic liner if desired, and mix together beer, chili sauce and onion soup mix. Add roast and turn to coat with sauce. Cook on LOW 6-8 hours or until tender.

NUTRITIONAL INFO:

Calories 346
Calories from Fat 24%
Fat 9g
Saturated Fat 4g
Cholesterol 111mg
Sodium 877mg
Carbohydrates 12g
Dietary Fiber 0g
Total Sugars 8g
Protein 449g
Dietary Exchanges:
1 other carbohydrate, 6 lean meat

TERRIFIC TIP

If not using a slow cooker, bake 325°F. about 4 hours or until tender.

Don't confuse Chili Sauce (found by mayo and dressings section of grocery) with Asian "hot" chili sauce or you'll have a very spicy recipe.

Season roast the day before and refrigerate, if time permitted.

BEEF BRISKET/BEEF SLIDERS

Four simple ingredients plus meat combine for a melt-in-your-mouth brisket meal that basically cooks itself!

Serves 16-20 (4-5 ounce) servings

1 (5-6 pound) brisket

Garlic Powder

2/3 cup light brown sugar

1 cup water

1 envelope dry onion soup mix

1 cup ketchup

1 Season brisket heavily with garlic powder. In 3 1/2-6-quart slow cooker, insert plastic liner if desired, and mix together remaining ingredients. Add brisket and turn to coat with sauce. Cook on LOW 6-8 hours or until tender.

NUTRITIONAL INFO:

Calories 302

Calories from Fat 35%

Fat 12g

Saturated Fat 4g

Cholesterol 105mg

Sodium 357mg

Carbohydrates 14g

Dietary Fiber 0g

Total Sugars 13g

Protein 34g

Dietary Exchanges:
1 other carbohydrate,
4 lean meat

TERRIFIC TIP

You can always toss in some potatoes, sweet potatoes and carrots, if desired.

For Beef Sliders: Fill miniature rolls with brisket, Brie, and red onion — easy and fantastic!

CABBAGE ROLL CASSEROLE

All the components of cabbage rolls combined into this delectable effortless casserole. A real winner!

  D

Makes 8 (1-cup) servings

1 1/2 pounds ground sirloin

1 onion, chopped

1 teaspoon minced garlic

1/4 teaspoon pepper

3 cups instant brown rice

1 (16-ounce) bag cole slaw

1 (24-26-ounce) jar healthy marinara sauce

1/4 cup light brown sugar

1 In 3 1/2-6 quart slow cooker, insert plastic liner if desired. In large skillet, cook meat, onion, and garlic over medium heat until meat is done, about 7 minutes. Drain any excess liquid. Add pepper.

2 Add meat with remaining ingredients to slow cooker. Cook on LOW 4-6 hours.

NUTRITIONAL INFO:

Calories 359

Calories from Fat 19%

Fat 8g

Saturated Fat 2g

Cholesterol 47mg

Sodium 396mg

Carbohydrates 48g

Dietary Fiber 5g

Total Sugars 16g

Protein 23g

Dietary Exchanges:
3 starch, 1 vegetable, 2 1/2 lean meat

TERRIFIC TIP

Don't Peek — Keep the lid on the slow cooker because every time you open the lid, you release heat and moisture and add 30 minutes to the cooking time.

MEATY LASAGNA

Makes a moist lasagna: keeps warm until ready to serve.

Makes 8-10 servings

1 1/4 pounds ground sirloin

1 onion, chopped

1 teaspoon minced garlic

1 teaspoon dried basil leaves

1 teaspoon dried oregano leaves

1 (24-ounce) jar marinara sauce

1/2 cup water

1 (15-ounce) container part-skim ricotta cheese

1 egg white

1 1/2 cups shredded part-skim mozzarella cheese

1 (8-ounce) box lasagna noodles

1 In large nonstick skillet, cook meat, onion, and garlic until meat is done. Drain any excess liquid. Add basil, oregano, marinara sauce and water.

2 In small bowl, mix ricotta, egg white and mozzarella.

3 In 3 1/2-6-quart slow cooker, insert plastic liner if desired, and layer 1 cup meat sauce, half the noodles (broken in pieces to make fit), and half the cheese mixture. Cover with 2 cups meat sauce, remaining noodles, and cheese mixture. Top with remaining meat sauce. Cook on HIGH 4 hours or until pasta is done.

NUTRITIONAL INFO:

Calories 301

Calories from Fat 30%

Fat 10g

Saturated Fat 5g

Cholesterol 59mg

Sodium 486mg

Carbohydrates 29g

Dietary Fiber 2g

Total Sugars 10g

Protein 25g

Dietary Exchanges:
1 1/2 starch, 1 vegetable, 3 1/2 lean meat

TERRIFIC TIP

If you want to sprinkle with more mozzarella on top, you can during the last 5 minutes of cooking.

BEEF FAJITAS

Wonderfully seasoned fall-apart tender meat makes the best fajitas. Serve with your favorite condiments and tortillas.

Makes 8 (about 1/2-cup meat) servings

2 pounds flat iron steak

2 (1-ounce) packets fajita seasoning mix

1 large onion, sliced

3 bell peppers, seeded and sliced (any combination green, red, yellow)

1/2 cup water

2 tablespoons red wine vinegar

1 In 3 1/2-6-quart slow cooker, insert plastic liner if desired, and add meat. Add remaining ingredients.

2 Cook on LOW 8 hours, or HIGH 5-6 hours or until tender. Use slotted spoon, to remove meat, onions and pepper.

NUTRITIONAL INFO:
Calories 227
Calories from Fat 41%
Fat 10g
Saturated Fat 3g
Cholesterol 79mg
Sodium 690mg
Carbohydrates 9g
Dietary Fiber 1g
Total Sugars 3g
Protein 23g
Dietary Exchanges:
1 vegetable,
3 lean meat

SNAZZY POTATOES & CARROTS

Slightly sweet and flavorsome. Fingerling potatoes come in different colors with slightly different flavors, and make a great presentation.

Makes 8 servings

2 pounds fingerling potatoes

1 pound bag baby carrots

1 large onion, chopped

1 cup fat-free vegetable or chicken broth

3 tablespoons light brown sugar

2 tablespoons butter

1 tablespoon olive oil

Salt and pepper to taste

1 In 3 1/2-6-quart slow cooker, insert plastic liner if desired, add potatoes, carrots and onion. Combine remaining ingredients in microwave safe-bowl. Microwave 1 minute or until brown sugar dissolves. Pour over potato mixture. Cook on HIGH 3 1/2-4 hours.

NUTRITIONAL INFO:
Calories 182
Calories from Fat 23%
Fat 5g
Saturated Fat 2g
Cholesterol 8mg
Sodium 335mg
Carbohydrates 33g
Dietary Fiber 5g
Total Sugars 10g
Protein 3g
Dietary Exchanges:
2 starch, 1 veg, 1/2 fat

BEST BEEF SHORT RIBS

We devoured this delicious dish with phenomenal gravy. Serve with rice to take advantage of this rich tasting gravy.

Makes 8 (3-ounce) servings

1/4 cup all-purpose flour

1 teaspoon dried thyme leaves

1 teaspoon garlic powder

2 tablespoons light brown sugar

3 pounds boneless lean beef short ribs, trimmed of excess fat

1 (12-ounce) bottle dark beer

1 (10 3/4-ounce) can French onion soup

1 In resealable plastic bag, mix flour, thyme, garlic powder and brown sugar. Add beef ribs coating well.

2 In 3 1/2-6-quart slow cooker, insert plastic liner if desired, add seasoned meat. Pour beer and onion soup over meat. Cook on LOW 6-8 hours or until meat is tender.

NUTRITIONAL INFO:

Calories 314

Calories from Fat 47%

Fat 16g

Saturated Fat 7g

Cholesterol 81mg

Sodium 248mg

Carbohydrates 10g

Dietary Fiber 1g

Total Sugars 5g

Protein 27g

Dietary Exchanges:
1/2 starch, 3 lean meat, 1 fat

TERRIFIC TIP

Slow cookers range from 3-6 quarts. Oval-shape cookers are nice for larger cuts of meat, such as briskets and ribs.

If using a cooker larger than what's called for increase everything proportionately, making sure the cooker is at least half to no more than two-thirds full.

CUBAN PORK & BLACK BEANS

Thanks to Joann Townley for sharing with me this fabulously flavored dish that we all cleaned our plate eating.

Makes 8 servings

2 (1-pound) pork tenderloins

Garlic powder

2 onions, chopped

1 (15-ounce) can black bean soup

1 (15-ounce) can black beans, rinsed and drained

1 (10-ounce) can tomatoes and green chilies

1 tablespoon chopped jalapenos

2 tablespoons ground cumin

2 tablespoons lime juice

1 Season tenderloins heavily with garlic powder. In 3 1/2-6-quart slow cooker, insert plastic liner if desired, and mix together remaining ingredients. Add tenderloins and turn to coat with sauce. Cook on LOW 6-8 hours or until tender.

NUTRITIONAL INFO:

Calories 245

Calories from Fat 23%

Fat 6g

Saturated Fat 2g

Cholesterol 76mg

Sodium 527mg

Carbohydrates 17g

Dietary Fiber 5g

Total Sugars 5g

Protein 29g

Dietary Exchanges:
1 starch, 1 vegetable, 4 lean meat

TERRIFIC TIP

Serving Option:
Serve over
yellow rice.

PORK TENDERLOIN
with PEANUT SAUCE

Fantastic fork tender pork with this marvelous peanutty sauce is a home run dinner. Top with crunchy peanuts and lime wedges for a fabulous finish.

Makes 6 servings

1 onion, thinly sliced

2 (1-pound) pork tenderloins

1/4 cup light brown sugar

1/4 cup low-sodium soy sauce

1 teaspoon minced garlic

1/3 cup creamy peanut butter

2 tablespoons chopped peanuts, optional

Lime wedges, optional

1 In 3 1/2-6-quart slow cooker, insert plastic liner if desired. Place onion slices into bottom of slow cooker and top with pork tenderloins. Add brown sugar, soy sauce, garlic, and peanut butter.

2 Cook on LOW 6-8 hours, or on HIGH 4-6 hours. About one hour before serving (if can), turn tenderloin over. Serve with chopped peanuts and lime wedges, if desired.

NUTRITIONAL INFO:

Calories 335

Calories from Fat 38%

Fat 14g

Saturated Fat 4g

Cholesterol 100mg

Sodium 401mg

Carbohydrates 16g

Dietary Fiber 1g

Total Sugars 13g

Protein 37g

Dietary Exchanges:
1 other carbohydrate,
5 lean meat

TERRIFIC TIP

For most slow cooker recipes, there is no need to stir — slow cookers cook food with low heat.

If you leave the top off you can lose up to 20 degrees of cooking heat in as little as 2 minutes. A quick peek, may only change the temperature 1-2 degrees.

SOUTHWESTERN CHICKEN

Flavor, flavor, flavor describes this southwestern chicken dish. Serve over rice.

Makes 8 (1-cup) servings

1 1/2 cups fat-free chicken broth

1 (10-ounce) can diced tomatoes with green chilies

1 (15-ounce) can black beans, rinsed and drained

1/2 cup chopped red onion

2 cups frozen corn

1 teaspoon ground cumin

1 teaspoon garlic powder

2 pounds boneless, skinless chicken breasts

1 bunch green onions, chopped

Salt and pepper to taste

1 In 3 1/2-6-quart slow cooker, insert plastic liner if desired and combine all ingredients except green onions in slow cooker. Cook on LOW 6-8 hours.

2 Remove chicken breasts and shred with two forks. Return shredded chicken to slow cooker. Add green onions and season to taste.

NUTRITIONAL INFO:

Calories 233

Calories from Fat 15%

Fat 4g

Saturated Fat 1g

Cholesterol 73mg

Sodium 600mg

Carbohydrates 20g

Dietary Fiber 5g

Total Sugars 3g

Protein 29g

Dietary Exchanges:
1 1/2 starch,
4 lean meat

TERRIFIC TIP

Try serving with cheese and a dollop of sour cream.

SESAME HONEY CHICKEN

 **D**

NUTRITIONAL INFO:

Calories 338

Calories from Fat 15%

Fat 6g

Saturated Fat 1g

Cholesterol 97mg

Sodium 550mg

Carbohydrates 40g

Dietary Fiber 1g

Total Sugars 36g

Protein 34g

Dietary Exchanges:
2 1/2 other
carbohydrate,
4 1/2 lean meat

TERRIFIC TIP

You can buy toasted sesame seeds in spice section. To toast sesame seeds, put in toaster oven or bake at 350°F several minutes — either way watch carefully as toasts quickly and burns easily (speaking from experience).

A touch of sweet with a touch of heat in this exceptionally wonderful chicken dish. Serve over rice.

Makes about 6 (2/3-cup) servings

2/3 cup honey

1/4 low-sodium soy sauce

1/4 cup ketchup

1 teaspoon olive oil

1 onion, chopped

1 teaspoon minced garlic

1/4 teaspoon red pepper flakes

2 pounds boneless, skinless chicken breasts

2 tablespoons cornstarch dissolved in 1/2 cup water

1 tablespoon sesame seeds, toasted

1 In 3 1/2-6-quart slow cooker, insert plastic liner if desired, or coat slow cooker with nonstick cooking spray. Add honey, soy sauce, ketchup, oil, onion, garlic and pepper. Add chicken and mix with sauce. Cook on LOW 4-6 hours or until chicken is tender.

2 Remove chicken to plate, leaving sauce in slow cooker. In small cup, combine cornstarch and water, mixing well. Pour into slow cooker; stirring into sauce. Cover and cook sauce on HIGH 10 minutes or until slightly thickened.

3 Cut chicken into bite size pieces and return to pot, stirring. Sprinkle with sesame seeds and serve.

BALSAMIC CHICKEN

Thanks to Donna Caro for her richly flavored and herby chicken dish.

Makes 6 servings

2 pounds boneless, skinless chicken breasts

Salt and pepper to taste

1 onion, thinly sliced

1 (14-ounce) can small artichokes, drained

2 (14 1/2-ounce) cans diced fire-roasted tomatoes

1 teaspoon minced garlic

1 teaspoon dried oregano leaves

1 teaspoon dried basil leaves

1 teaspoon dried rosemary leaves

1/2 teaspoon dried thyme leaves

1/2 cup balsamic vinegar

1 In 3 1/2-6-quart slow cooker, insert liner into slow cooker, if desired. Season chicken to taste and place in slow cooker. Top with onion and artichokes. In a bowl, combine remaining ingredients and pour over chicken.

2 Cook on LOW 6-8 hours or HIGH 4-5 hours.

NUTRITIONAL INFO:

Calories 239

Calories from Fat 15%

Fat 4g

Saturated Fat 1g

Cholesterol 97mg

Sodium 600mg

Carbohydrates 15g

Dietary Fiber 3g

Total Sugars 8g

Protein 34g

Dietary Exchanges:
3 vegetable,
4 lean meat

TERRIFIC TIP

Serve over pasta, rice, or couscous to take advantage of the wonderful sauce.

CHICKEN & SAUSAGE JAMBALAYA

Give our Cajun favorite one-pot meal a try. Just prep the ingredients, plug in the cooker, and you'll be good to go.

Makes 8 (1 1/2-cup) servings

1 pound boneless, skinless chicken breast, cut into chunks

1/2 pound reduced-fat sausage, sliced

1 cup chopped celery

1 large onion, chopped

1 green pepper, seeded and chopped

1 teaspoon minced garlic

1/2 teaspoon dried thyme leaves

1 (14-ounce) can diced tomatoes

2 cups fat-free chicken broth

2 tablespoons tomato paste

Salt and pepper to taste

2 cups instant brown rice

1/2 chopped green onions

1 In 3 1/2-6-quart slow cooker, insert plastic liner if desired and place chicken and sausage in slow cooker. Add remaining ingredients except brown rice and green onions.

2 Cook on LOW 2 1/2 hours. Turn to HIGH and stir in rice and green onions. Cover, and cook 30 minutes more or until rice is tender and liquid absorbed.

NUTRITIONAL INFO:

Calories 220

Calories from Fat 13%

Fat 3g

Saturated Fat 1g

Cholesterol 46mg

Sodium 652mg

Carbohydrates 28g

Dietary Fiber 3g

Total Sugars 6g

Protein 19g

Dietary Exchanges:
1 1/2 starch,
1 vegetable,
2 1/2 lean meat

TERRIFIC TIP

Use low-sodium chicken broth for diabetic friendly recipe.

Look for a healthier version turkey Andouille sausage.

Tired of wasting tomato paste, buy it in a tube — squeeze out desired amount!

BREAKFAST CASSEROLE

Wake up in the morning to this fabulous one-pot breakfast with sweet potato tater tots, ham, onion, and green pepper.

Makes 8 (3/4-cup) servings

1 pound frozen sweet potato crisp bite size puffs (tater tots)

1 (6-ounce) package Canadian bacon, diced

1 onion, chopped

1 green bell pepper, seeded and chopped

1 1/4 cups shredded reduced-fat sharp Cheddar cheese

4 eggs

3 egg whites

1/2 cup skim milk

Salt and pepper to taste

1 In 3 1/2-6-quart slow cooker, insert plastic liner, if desired. Depending on size of slow cooker, layer tater tots, Canadian bacon, onion, green pepper and cheese two or three times.

2 In bowl, whisk together eggs, egg whites and milk. Season to taste. Pour egg mixture over layers in slow cooker. Cook on LOW 5-8 hours or until egg mixture is set.

NUTRITIONAL INFO:
Calories 235
Calories from Fat 45%
Fat 12g
Saturated Fat 4g
Cholesterol 114mg
Sodium 740mg
Carbohydrates 16g
Dietary Fiber 2g
Total Sugars 3g
Protein 15g
Dietary Exchanges:
1 starch, 2 lean meat, 1 fat

TERRIFIC TIP

For a vegetarian option, omit Canadian bacon. If desired, when done, you can sprinkle more cheese on top (if you like more cheese).

BBQ SHRIMP

 D

NUTRITIONAL INFO:

Calories 179

Calories from Fat 53%

Fat 10g

Saturated Fat 1g

Cholesterol 125mg

Sodium 534mg

Carbohydrates 7g

Dietary Fiber 1g

Total Sugars 2g

Protein 14g

Dietary Exchanges:
1/2 other carbohydrate,
2 lean meat, 1 fat

OMG — this delectable sauce you can eat with a spoon so pick-up French bread to soak it up. This is a get your hands dirty recipe as peeling shrimp is messy but fun with unbelievable flavor.

Makes 6-8 servings

2 pounds medium-large shrimp, shells on (21-25 per pound)

1/3 cup olive oil

1/3 cup Worcestershire sauce

1/2 cup fat-free Italian dressing

2 tablespoons lemon juice

1 tablespoon minced garlic

2 teaspoons hot sauce

1 tablespoon paprika

1 tablespoon dried oregano leaves

1 tablespoon dried basil leaves

1 In 3 1/2-6-quart slow cooker, insert plastic liner if desired, and mix in all ingredients. Cook on HIGH 2 hours, or until shrimp are done (turn opaque and peel easily).

PULLED PORK SHOULDER

Get ready for a mouth-watering taste sensation.

Makes 6 servings

1 medium onion, chopped

1 teaspoon ground ginger

2 teaspoons minced garlic

2 cups diet cola

1/2 cup hoisin sauce

1/3 cup seasoned rice vinegar

1/3 cup low-sodium soy sauce

1 (3-pound) bone in pork shoulder roast

1 tablespoon cornstarch dissolved in 1/4 cup water

1 In 3 1/2-6-quart slow cooker, insert plastic liner if desired, and mix together onion, ginger, garlic, cola, hoisin sauce, rice vinegar, and soy sauce. Add roast. Cook on LOW 6-8 hours.

2 Remove pork roast to plate, leaving sauce in slow cooker. Turn to HIGH. In small cup, mix cornstarch and water. Pour into slow cooker; stirring into sauce. Cover and cook sauce 10 minutes or until slightly thickened. Shred pork roast with two forks. Spoon sauce over meat.

NUTRITIONAL INFO:

Calories 302

Calories from Fat 32%

Fat 10g

Saturated Fat 4g

Cholesterol 111mg

Sodium 783mg

Carbohydrates 16g

Dietary Fiber 1g

Total Sugars 12g

Protein 35g

Dietary Exchanges:
1 other carbohydrate,
5 lean meat

TERRIFIC TIP

Great by itself, or try it on a delicious bun or in a wrap topped with slaw!

BANANAS FOSTER

Thanks to Lisa Guilino for this Louisiana favorite recipe.

Makes 7 (1/3-cup servings)

1/4 cup butter, melted

1/3 cup light brown sugar

1/4 teaspoon ground cinnamon

6 fresh bananas, cut into 1-inch slices

1/4 cup crème de banana, rum or orange juice

1 In 3 1/2-6-quart slow cooker, insert plastic liner if desired. Add butter, brown sugar and cinnamon; stir. Add in bananas and crème de banana. Cook on LOW one hour.

NUTRITIONAL INFO:

Calories 255

Calories from Fat 26%

Fat 7g

Saturated Fat 4g

Cholesterol 17mg

Sodium 62mg

Carbohydrates 38g

Dietary Fiber 3g

Total Sugars 27g

Protein 1g

Dietary Exchanges:
1 1/2 fruit, 1 other carbohydrate, 1 1/2 fat

COCONUT CAKE

Ever want to eat a cake hot from the oven? Now you can have your wish! Thought it would be fun to try a cake in my crock pot and this moist coconut cake rocks!

Makes 16 servings

1 (18.25-ounce) box yellow cake mix

1/4 cup canola oil

2 eggs

2 egg whites

1 teaspoon coconut extract

1 1/3 cups lite coconut milk, divided

2 tablespoons confectioners' sugar

1/4 cup flaked coconut

1 In 3 1/2-6-quart slow cooker, insert plastic liner if desired, or coat with nonstick cooking spray.

2 In bowl, combine cake mix, oil, eggs, egg whites, coconut extract and 1 cup coconut milk, mixing well. Transfer to slow cooker, cook on HIGH about 1 hour 15 minutes (if using 4 quart crock pot, will take about 2 hours).

3 When cake is done, Whisk together remaining 1/3 cup coconut milk with confectioners' sugar, mixing well. Poke holes in hot cake with toothpick; gradually pour coconut milk over top of cake. Sprinkle with coconut and serve.

NUTRITIONAL INFO:

Calories 192

Calories from Fat 37%

Fat 8g

Saturated Fat 2g

Cholesterol 23mg

Sodium 237mg

Carbohydrates 28g

Dietary Fiber 0g

Total Sugars 15g

Protein 3g

Dietary Exchanges:
2 other carbohydrate,
1 1/2 fat

FUDGY BROWNIES

If you like fudgy ooey gooey brownies, get the crock-pot going, and a bite of chocolate decadence will be ready while you get your errands done.

Makes 16-24 brownies

1 (18.3-ounce) package brownie mix

1/4 cup canola oil

1 egg

1/4 cup water

1/2 (14-ounce) can fat-free sweetened condensed milk

1/2 cup chopped pecans

3/4 cup old-fashioned oatmeal

1 In 3 1/2-6-quart slow cooker, insert plastic liner if desired, and coat with nonstick cooking spray. In large bowl, stir together brownie mix, oil, egg and water until well combined. Transfer brownie mixture to lined slow cooker.

2 Carefully spread half the can of sweetened condensed milk over brownie mixture. Top with pecans and oatmeal; don't stir. Cook on HIGH 3 hours or until done and edges pull away from sides.

NUTRITIONAL INFO:

Calories 167

Calories from Fat 37%

Fat 7g

Saturated Fat 1g

Cholesterol 9mg

Sodium 75mg

Carbohydrates 24g

Dietary Fiber 0g

Total Sugars 16g

Protein 2g

Dietary Exchanges:
1 1/2 other carbohydrate, 1 1/2 fat

TERRIFIC TIP

Make it easy on yourself, especially cleanup, by using plastic slow cooker liners. These fit most 3 1/2-6 quart oval and round slow cookers.

Chocolicious Peanut Butter Dessert (pg 176)

8

SWEET TEMPTATIONS

STRAWBERRY CHEESECAKE PARFAITS

A fabulous no-cook dessert! This berry and cheesecake combination creates an explosion of flavor for cheesecake fans.

Makes 8 parfaits

1 pound strawberries, stemmed and sliced

1 tablespoon sugar

1 (8-ounce) package reduced-fat cream cheese

1/2 cup plain or vanilla nonfat Greek yogurt

1/2 cup confectioners' sugar

1 teaspoon almond extract

1 1/2 cups frozen nonfat whipped topping, thawed, divided

2/3 cup graham cracker crumbs

Mint, garnish, optional

1 In bowl, sprinkle strawberries with sugar, toss and set aside

2 In mixing bowl, beat cream cheese, yogurt, confectioners sugar and almond extract until smooth. Fold in 1/2 cup whipped topping.

3 To assemble parfaits, in small dish or glass, layer graham cracker crumbs, cream cheese filling, and strawberries. Repeat layers if small enough dish and end with dollop of whipped topping. Garnish with mint, if desired.

NUTRITIONAL INFO:

Calories 188

Calories from Fat 34%

Fat 7g

Saturated Fat 4g

Cholesterol 20mg

Sodium 170mg

Carbohydrates 25g

Dietary Fiber 1g

Total Sugars 17g

Protein 6g

Dietary Exchanges:
1 1/2 other carbohydrate, 1 lean meat, 1 fat

TERRIFIC TIP

Any berries or a combination may be used.

Any time a recipe calls for yogurt or Greek yogurt, either is fine. I like Greek yogurt as it is a richer, creamier and thicker yogurt, especially in this dessert-but make sure to get vanilla flavor.

CHOCOLATE DECADENCE

A chocolate miracle in minutes –this is too good for words. Don't fret if the pieces fall apart a little - as it looks like chocolate bark. Who doesn't love sweet and salty?

Makes 72 (1-piece) candies

2 cups semisweet chocolate chips

1 (4-ounce) bar German chocolate

1/2 cup peanut butter

1 cup coarsely chopped pecans

2 cups coarsely chopped pretzels

4 cups miniature marshmallows

1 Line 11x7x2-inch baking pan with foil or parchment paper coated with nonstick cooking spray.

2 In large microwave-safe dish, combine chocolate chips, German chocolate and peanut butter. Microwave 2 minutes; stir until smooth. Stir in pecans, pretzels and marshmallows. Spread and press into prepared pan.

3 Freeze 15-20 minutes or until firm enough to cut. Invert chocolate slab on cutting board, remove foil and invert again. Cut into small squares or pieces. Keep in refrigerator in airtight container or plastic bags.

NUTRITIONAL INFO:

Calories 77

Calories from Fat 46%

Fat 4g

Saturated Fat 2g

Cholesterol 0mg

Sodium 51mg

Carbohydrates 10g

Dietary Fiber 1g

Total Sugars 6g

Protein 1g

Dietary Exchanges:
1/2 other carbohydrate, 1 fat

CHOCOLICIOUS PEANUT BUTTER DESSERT

A "worth fighting for" easy and divine dessert with magical layers.

Makes 20 servings

NUTRITIONAL INFO:

Calories 192

Calories from Fat 43%

Fat 9g

Saturated Fat 4g

Cholesterol 13mg

Sodium 244mg

Carbohydrates 24g

Dietary Fiber 1g

Total Sugars 15g

Protein 3g

Dietary Exchanges: 1 1/2 other carbohydrate, 2 fat

TERRIFIC TIP

When a recipe calls for peanut butter, use crunchy or smooth — whatever is in your pantry.

You can top with crushed peanut butter cups, also.

1 1/4 cups chocolate sandwich cream cookie crumbs (about 24 cookies)

3 tablespoons butter, melted

1 (8-ounce) package reduced-fat cream cheese

1/3 cup creamy peanut butter

2/3 cup confectioners' sugar

1 (8-ounce) container frozen nonfat whipped topping, thawed, divided

1 cup skim milk

1 (4-serving) box instant chocolate fudge pudding and pie filling mix

Crushed chocolate sandwich cream cookies, optional

1 In small bowl, mix together cookie crumbs and butter. Press into 13x9x2-inch dish; set aside.

2 In mixing bowl, beat cream cheese, peanut butter and confectioners' sugar until smooth. Fold in 3/4 cup whipped topping. Carefully spread over crust.

3 In another large bowl, whisk together milk and pudding mix until creamy. Let stand 2 minutes until thickened. Fold in another 3/4 cup whipped topping into pudding.

4 Carefully spread pudding mixture over peanut butter layer. Top with remaining whipped topping, a thin layer. Sprinkle with crushed cookies, if desired. Cover and chill for at least 3 hours.

CHOCOLATE CHIP OATMEAL PEANUT BUTTER COOKIES

All my favorite ingredients wrapped up into one outrageous cookie.

Makes 3 dozen cookies

2 tablespoons butter

1/4 cup canola oil

2/3 cup light brown sugar

1/2 cup peanut butter (creamy or crunchy)

1 teaspoon vanilla extract

1 egg

1 cup all-purpose flour

1 teaspoon baking soda

1 cup old-fashioned oatmeal

1/2 cup semisweet or dark chocolate chips

1 Preheat oven 350° F. Coat baking sheet with nonstick cooking spray.

2 In mixing bowl, mix together butter, oil, and brown sugar until blended. Add peanut butter, vanilla and egg, mixing well.

3 In another bowl, combine flour and baking soda. Gradually add flour mixture to peanut butter mixture, mixing only until combined. Stir in oatmeal and chocolate chips. Drop dough by spoonfuls onto baking sheets. Bake 10 minutes or until cookie edges begin to brown.

NUTRITIONAL INFO:

Calories 95

Calories from Fat 47%

Fat 5g

Saturated Fat 1g

Cholesterol 7mg

Sodium 60mg

Carbohydrates 11g

Dietary Fiber 1g

Total Sugars 6g

Protein 2g

Dietary Exchanges:
1/2 other carbohydrate, 1 fat

TERRIFIC TIP

Most baked cookies and cakes freeze very well, up to 6 months.

RED VELVET CHEESECAKE

Two popular desserts, red velvet cake and cheesecake create the ultimate indulgence.

Makes 2 (9-inch round) cheesecake pies — 16 servings

2 (8-ounce) packages reduced-fat cream cheese

1 1/4 cups sugar

2 eggs

1 egg white

1 tablespoon cornstarch

3 tablespoon cocoa

1 cup nonfat sour cream

1 teaspoon vanilla extract

1/2 cup buttermilk

1 teaspoon vinegar

1 (1-ounce) bottle red food coloring

2 (9-inch) round commercially bought chocolate pie crusts

1 Preheat oven 350° F.

2 In mixing bowl, beat cream cheese and sugar until creamy. Add eggs, egg white, cornstarch, cocoa, sour cream, vanilla, buttermilk, vinegar and red food coloring, mixing well.

3 Pour into crust. Bake 35-40 minutes or until center is firm. Turn off oven and remain in oven 30 minutes. Cover and refrigerate until well chilled.

NUTRITIONAL INFO:

Calories 270

Calories from Fat 39%

Fat 12g

Saturated Fat 5g

Cholesterol 46mg

Sodium 262mg

Carbohydrates 34g

Dietary Fiber 1g

Total Sugars 23g

Protein 7g

Dietary Exchanges:
2 1/2 other carbohydrate, 2 1/2 fat

TERRIFIC TIP

For chocolate crust: 1 1/4 cups chocolate, 1 tablespoon sugar, 1/2 teaspoon vanilla extract, 2 tablespoons butter melted, combine all, press into bottom of spring form pan, and bake 350°F 10 minutes.

COOKIES & CREAM CHEESECAKE CUPCAKES

A cupcake with two favorites, Oreo cookies and cheesecake, easy to make and incredibly delicious.

Makes 20 cheesecake cupcakes

20 chocolate sandwich cream cookies

2 (8-ounce) packages reduced-fat cream cheese

1/2 cup sugar

1 egg

2 egg whites

1/2 cup nonfat plain Greek yogurt

1 teaspoon vanilla extract

6 crushed chocolate sandwich cream cookies

1 Preheat oven 300°F. Line muffin pan with paper liners.

2 Place one whole cookie in the bottom of each cupcake paper.

3 In mixing bowl, beat cream cheese and sugar until light. Gradually add egg and egg whites beating until creamy. Add yogurt and vanilla, mixing well. Stir in crushed cookies.

4 Divide batter between cookie filled cups. Bake 25-28 minutes or until filling set. Cool and refrigerate in pan about 2 hours.

NUTRITIONAL INFO:

Calories 154

Calories from Fat 47%

Fat 8g

Saturated Fat 4g

Cholesterol 25mg

Sodium 186mg

Carbohydrates 16g

Dietary Fiber 0g

Total Sugars 11g

Protein 4g

Dietary Exchanges:
1 other carbohydrate, 1 1/2 fat

TERRIFIC TIP

A great make ahead treat as cheesecakes freeze well.

BROWNIES *with* PEANUT BUTTER OATMEAL CRUMBLE

 D

NUTRITIONAL INFO:

Calories 106

Calories from Fat 46%

Fat 5g

Saturated Fat 1g

Cholesterol 9mg

Sodium 52mg

Carbohydrates 13g

Dietary Fiber 0g

Total Sugars 8g

Protein 2g

Dietary Exchanges:
1 other carbohydrate,
1 fat

An intoxicating combination of a luscious brownie, peanut butter and oatmeal all together in one bite.

Makes 48 brownies

1 (18.25-ounce) box brownie mix

1/3 cup canola oil

1/4 cup water

2 eggs

1/2 cup peanut butter (crunchy or creamy)

2 tablespoons butter

1/3 cup light brown sugar

1 cup old-fashioned oatmeal

2 tablespoons all-purpose flour

1/3 cup semisweet chocolate chips

1 Preheat oven 350°F. Line 13x9x2-inch baking pan with foil and coat with nonstick cooking spray.

2 In large bowl, mix together brownie mix, oil, water and eggs until well combined. Transfer to prepared pan.

3 In microwave-safe bowl, microwave peanut butter and butter one minute; stir until melted. Stir in brown sugar, oatmeal and flour until combined. Sprinkle and gently press peanut butter mixture over brownie layer. Sprinkle with chocolate chips. Bake 20 minutes or until top is soft to touch.

S'MORES COOKIES

This camping favorite transforms into a melt-in-your-mouth s'mores cookie.

Makes 60 cookies

1/2 cup butter, softened

1 cup light brown sugar

1/4 cup sugar

2 eggs

1 teaspoon vanilla extract

1 1/2 cups all-purpose flour

1 cup graham cracker crumbs

1 teaspoon baking soda

1/2 teaspoon cinnamon

1 1/2 cups mini marshmallows

4 ounces chocolate candy bars, broken into small pieces.

NUTRITIONAL INFO:
Calories 65
Calories from Fat 33%
Fat 2g
Saturated Fat 1g
Cholesterol 11mg
Sodium 46mg
Carbohydrates 10g
Dietary Fiber 0g
Total Sugars 7g
Protein 1g
Dietary Exchanges:
1/2 other carbohydrate, 1/2 fat

1 Preheat oven 350°F. Coat baking sheet with nonstick cooking spray.

2 In mixing bowl, beat butter and both sugars until light and fluffy. Add eggs and vanilla mixing until combined.

3 In another bowl, combine flour, graham cracker crumbs, baking soda, and cinnamon. Gradually add flour mixture, mixing until well combined. Fold in marshmallows and chocolate pieces.

4 Drop by teaspoonful on prepared pan. Bake 8-10 minutes or until golden brown. Cool 10 minutes before removing from pan.

CHOCOLATE ITALIAN CREAM CAKE

TERRIFIC TIP

*If can't find Butter
Pecan Cake mix,
substitute butter
cake mix.*

*If you don't like
coconut, like my
sister, you can
leave it out.*

*And, no time to
toast the pecans,
then don't as I
toast them just to
intensify the flavor.*

One of the easiest, most extraordinary, and absolutely delicious cakes you can make — my personal favorite!

Makes 16-20 servings

1 (18.25-ounce) box Butter Pecan Cake mix

1/4 cup cocoa

1/3 cup canola oil

2 eggs

2 egg whites

1 1/4 cups water

1 teaspoon coconut extract

1/2 cup chopped pecans, toasted

1/2 cup flaked coconut

Chocolate Cream Cheese Icing (recipe follows)

Toasted coconut and pecans, optional (about 2 tablespoons each)

1 Preheat oven 350°F. Coat three 9-inch pans with nonstick cooking spray.

2 In mixing bowl, beat together cake mix, cocoa, oil, eggs, egg whites, water and coconut extract. Stir in pecans and coconut.

3 Pour batter evenly into prepared pans. Bake 12-15 minutes, until tops spring back when touched. Cool 10 minutes and turn out onto cooling racks.

4 Frost layers and sides with Chocolate Cream Cheese Icing (see recipe) and sprinkle with toasted coconut and pecans, if desired.

CHOCOLATE CREAM CHEESE ICING

1 (8-ounce) package reduced-fat cream cheese

3 tablespoons butter

1/4 cup cocoa

1 (16-ounce) box confectioners' sugar

1 teaspoon vanilla extract

1 In bowl, beat cream cheese and butter until smooth. Gradually add cocoa and confectioners' sugar, mixing until creamy. Add vanilla.

Chocolate Italian Cream Cake (pg 182)

NO-BAKE GERMAN CHOCOLATE MOUNDS

These German chocolate and oatmeal trouble-free cookies are sure to cure that impulsive last minute sweet tooth.

Makes 30 chocolate mounds

6 tablespoons butter

1/2 cup sugar

1/4 cup cocoa

1/2 cup skim milk

1 cup mini marshmallows

1 teaspoon vanilla extract

1/2 teaspoon coconut extract

2 cups old-fashioned oatmeal

1/2 cup chopped pecans

1/3 cup flaked coconut

1 In nonstick pot, combine butter, sugar, cocoa, milk, and marshmallows, cooking over low heat, stirring until smooth and marshmallows dissolved.

2 Bring to boil and boil 2 minutes. Remove from heat and cool slightly. Stir in vanilla and coconut extracts, oatmeal, pecans and coconut.

3 Drop by teaspoonfuls onto waxed paper lined baking sheet. Refrigerate until firm.

NUTRITIONAL INFO:

Calories 80

Calories from Fat 47%

Fat 4g

Saturated Fat 2g

Cholesterol 6mg

Sodium 26mg

Carbohydrates 10g

Dietary Fiber 1g

Total Sugars 5g

Protein 1g

Dietary Exchanges:
1/2 other
carbohydrate, 1 fat

TERRIFIC TIP

Freeze on baking sheet until hardened and then transfer to zip-top plastic bags to store easily.

LEMONADE CAKE

This luscious lemon cake, with a light lemon flavor, hits the spot.

Makes 16-20 servings

6 tablespoons butter

1 1/3 cups sugar

2 eggs

2 egg whites

1/4 cup frozen lemonade concentrate, thawed

1 teaspoon vanilla extract

2 cups all-purpose flour

1 teaspoon baking powder

1/2 teaspoon baking soda

1 tablespoon grated lemon rind, optional

1 cup buttermilk

Lemonade Frosting (recipe follows)

1 Preheat oven 350°F. Coat two (9-inch) round cake pans with nonstick cooking spray.

2 In mixing bowl, beat together butter and sugar until well mixed. Add eggs and egg whites, one at a time, beating well after each addition. Add lemonade concentrate and vanilla.

3 In small bowl, combine flour, baking powder, baking soda, and lemon rind. Add flour mixture and buttermilk alternately to sugar mixture, beginning and ending with flour mixture.

4 Transfer batter into prepared pans. Bake 18-20 minutes or until wooden pick inserted in center comes out clean. Cool layers on wire racks. Ice with Lemonade Frosting (see recipe).

LEMONADE FROSTING

2 tablespoons butter

1 (8-ounce) package reduced-fat cream cheese

2 tablespoons frozen lemonade concentrate, thawed

1 (16-ounce) box confectioners' sugar

1 In mixing bowl, beat butter and cream cheese. Add lemonade concentrate. Gradually add confectioners' sugar until creamy.

NUTRITIONAL INFO:

Calories 280

Calories from Fat 25%

Fat 8g

Saturated Fat 5g

Cholesterol 39mg

Sodium 167mg

Carbohydrates 49g

Dietary Fiber 0g

Total Sugars 39g

Protein 4g

Dietary Exchanges:
3 other carbohydrate, 1 1/2 fat

TERRIFIC TIP

Use lemonade concentrate (small frozen lemonade) for cake, icing and then make yourself a drink with any left.

CARROT CAKE *with* CREAM CHEESE FROSTING

NUTRITIONAL INFO:
Calories 329
Calories from Fat 31%
Fat 12g
Saturated Fat 3g
Cholesterol 31mg
Sodium 243mg
Carbohydrates 53g
Dietary Fiber 2g
Total Sugars 41g
Protein 4g
Dietary Exchanges:
3 1/2 other
carbohydrate, 2 fat

As a carrot cake fan, I assure you that you will adore this amazing moist carrot cake with a hint of orange, and iced with a rich, creamy Cream Cheese Frosting.

Makes 16-20 servings

2 cups all-purpose flour

2 teaspoons baking soda

1 teaspoon baking powder

2 teaspoons ground cinnamon

2 eggs

2 egg whites

1/4 cup canola oil

1 1/2 cups sugar

1 cup orange juice

1 teaspoon vanilla extract

1 (1-pound) bag carrots, peeled and grated (about 2 1/2 cups)

1 cup chopped pecans

Cream Cheese Frosting (recipe follows)

1 Preheat oven 350°F. Coat two (9-inch) round pans with nonstick cooking spray.

2 In bowl, mix together flour, baking soda, baking powder and cinnamon; set aside.

3 In large mixing bowl, beat together eggs, egg whites, oil, sugar, orange juice, and vanilla. Gradually add flour mixture stirring until blended. Stir in carrots and pecans, mixing until combined.

4 Pour batter into prepared pans. Bake 25-30 minutes or until tops spring back when lightly touched. Cool 10 minutes; then turn out onto racks to cool. Frost layers and sides with Cream Cheese Frosting (see recipe).

CREAM CHEESE FROSTING

The touch of orange complements the cake.

1 (8-ounce) package reduced-fat cream cheese

3 tablespoons butter

1 teaspoon vanilla extract

1 tablespoon orange juice or as needed

1 (16-ounce) box confectioners' sugar

1 In mixing bowl beat together cream cheese and butter until smooth. Add vanilla and orange juice. Gradually add confectioners' sugar mixing until creamy.

TERRIFIC TIP

Add more or less orange juice until desired consistency.

CHOCOLATE PEANUT BUTTER TRIFLE

A make-ahead show stopper dessert — beyond good!

Makes 20 2/3-cup servings

2 (4-serving) boxes instant chocolate fudge pudding and pie filling mix

3 1/2 cups skim milk

1 (14-16-ounce) bought angel food cake, cut into cubes

Peanut Butter Cream Cheese Filling (recipe follows)

12 miniature peanut butter cups, crumbled, divided

1 (8-ounce) container frozen nonfat whipped topping, thawed

1 In bowl, whisk together chocolate pudding and milk according to package directions.

2 In trifle or large glass bowl, layer ingredients beginning with one-third angel food cake, one-half Peanut Butter Cream Cheese Filling (see recipe), half of chocolate pudding, one-third peanut butter cups, and whipped topping. Repeat layers ending with remaining third peanut butter cups.

PEANUT BUTTER FILLING

Makes 20 servings

1 (8-ounce) package reduced-fat cream cheese

1/2 cup creamy peanut butter

1/2 cup confectioners' sugar

2/3 cup skim milk

1 In mixing bowl, beat together cream cheese and peanut butter. Gradually add confectioners' sugar and milk mixing until creamy.

NUTRITIONAL INFO:

Calories 233

Calories from Fat 27%

Fat 7g

Saturated Fat 3g

Cholesterol 9mg

Sodium 330mg

Carbohydrates 36g

Dietary Fiber 1g

Total Sugars 25g

Protein 7g

Dietary Exchanges:
2 1/2 other carbohydrate, 1 1/2 fat

TERRIFIC TIP

If you don't have a trifle bowl, use a large glass bowl because you want to be able to see the layers for the presentation.

Chocolate Peanut Butter Trifle (pg 188)

INDEX